2/36

W9-CGY-353

Science as
Intellectual Property

No Longer Property of
Phillips Memorial Library

AAAS Series on Issues in Science and Technology

Published

Science as Intellectual Property: Who Controls Scientific Research?
Dorothy Nelkin

In Press

Biotechnology
Philip Abelson, Editor

Science Education in Global Perspective: Lessons from Five Countries
Margrete S. Klein, F. James Rutherford, and Kathryn Wolff, editors

Science and Creation: Geological, Theological, and Educational Perspectives
Robert W. Hanson, Editor

Scientists and Journalists: Exploring the Connection
Sharon M. Friedman, Sharon Dunwoddy, and Carol Rogers, Editors

Science as Intellectual Property

Who Controls Research?

Dorothy Nelkin
Cornell University

AAAS Series on Issues in Science and Technology

MACMILLAN PUBLISHING COMPANY
A Division of Macmillan, Inc.
NEW YORK

Collier Macmillan Publishers
LONDON

Phillips Memorial
Library
Providence College

Copyright © 1984 by AAAS

All rights reserved. No part of this book may be reproduced or transmitted in any form or by any means, electronic or mechanical, including photocopying, recording, or by any information storage and retrieval system, without permission in writing from the Publisher.

Macmillan Publishing Company
866 Third Avenue, New York, N.Y. 10022

Collier Macmillan Canada, Inc.

Printed in the United States of America

printing number paperback
1 2 3 4 5 6 7 8 9 10

printing number hardcover
1 2 3 4 5 6 7 8 9 10

Library of Congress Cataloging in Publication Data

Nelkin, Dorothy.
  Science as intellectual property.

  (AAAS series on issues in science and technology)
  Bibliography: p.
  Includes index.
  1. Research—United States. 2. Science and state—
United States. 3. Communication in science—United
States. 4. Confidential communications—United States.
I. Title.   II. Series.
Q180.U5N37 1983   001.4   83-3805
ISBN 0-02-949080-4
ISBN 0-02-949090-1 (pbk.)

Contents

Foreword

Although the notion of knowledge as property cannot be called new, the scale of contemporary American scientific research is unsettling long-held assumptions and raising questions that promise to bedevil the field of science policy for years to come.

The emerging structure of the American research enterprise is no longer the simple trilateral alliance among academia, government and industry that, in the first postwar decades, operated on consensus and goodwill. Stage by stage, it has evolved into a pyramiding of partnerships running the gamut from the nostalgic sponsor-investigator relationship to strenuously negotiated agreements at the level of the macroinstitution. The immense reach of government dominates the research process even as corporate enterprise offers the relief of funding diversification to leading research universities, and the research scientist increasingly encounters dilemmas of rights, regulations, multiple sponsorship, professional conscience, openness, and secrecy. As infrastructure expands, dilemmas multiply.

The AAAS Committee on Scientific Freedom and Responsibility has no monopoly on perspectives towards these matters. On the other hand, the Committee is well placed to search for a framework against which the questions can be sorted out and examined. It is this task that Professor Nelkin has been willing to undertake, and she has addressed it with characteristic energy, reflection, and responsibility. In publishing her work, AAAS is moved both by its timeliness and its substantive contribution to the awareness of issues that touch deeply the process and the essential propositions on which the advancement of science depends.

William D. Carey
Executive Officer
American Association for the
Advancement of Science

Acknowledgements

This manuscript grew out of my involvement in the Committee on Scientific Freedom and Responsibility of the American Association for the Advancement of Science. I have greatly benefitted from research material generously provided by Rosemary Chalk and members of the committee who have commented in detail on various drafts of the paper. Special thanks for extensive review are due to Rosemary Chalk, Anna Harrison, Esther Hopkins, Elena Nightingale, and Harold Relyea. I have also gained invaluable suggestions on portions of the manuscript from Sissela Bok, Michael Brown, Stefan Dedijer, Robert Gellman, Edward Gerjuoy, David Goldwyn, Bradford Gray, Herman Pollak, Walter Lynn, Barbara Mishkin, and Lisa Norling. I began this research while a guest at the Laboratoire d'Econometrie of the Ecole Polytechnique in Paris. Their hospitality and the help of my colleagues at the Program on Science, Technology, and Society at Cornell are appreciated.

Science as
Intellectual Property

1. The Ownership and Control of Scientific Information

Questions about the control of research and scientific information are at the center of a growing number of legal and administrative disputes. The questions raise fundamental issues of professional sovereignty, scientific secrecy, and proprietary rights. For instance, do data belong to the scientist who does the research or to the federal agency that pays for it? What does government funding mean in terms of public access and investigator control? What means of access to scientific data are available to interested citizens, competing scientists, or industrial firms? Does the Freedom of Information Act apply to research that is in progress? At what point in the research process are data to be made available? Do demands for disclosure of data adequately respect the confidentiality of the sources and the privacy of the subjects of research? Can scientists themselves use their data and ideas in whatever way they choose?

Questions such as these have always been controversial because of the application of science to practical problems, its role in justifying policy decisions, and its importance in national affairs. However, several factors have recently complicated our understanding of the ownership and control of scientific information. In particular, the knowledge generated by research is growing in economic and policy importance. The findings of research may, for example, form the basis for decisions about whether a chemical product or a drug can be marketed and how it will be regulated. In the past, commercial interests looked primarily to the goods and services produced through applied research; today, more fundamental knowledge is also recognized as having intrinsic value.

Scientists have traditionally distinguished basic research, which is concerned primarily with the advancement of knowledge, from applied research, which is oriented toward the development of new products of commercial or military value; however, such distinctions are becoming blurred in several fields. The National Science Board calls its 1981 report "Only One Science," a phrase borrowed from Louis Pasteur: "There is only one science and the application of science, and these two activities are linked as the fruit is to the tree."[1] Indeed, the application of knowledge today is often immediate and direct, and research scientists themselves are personally involved in commercializing their work.

A variety of institutional and policy changes are further complicating the question of proprietary control over scientific information. Concerned about lagging industrial innovation and growing international competition, government officials are urging scientists to break down the organizational barriers between applied and basic research and between industrial and academic science. In the view of one congressional observer, "The only way to accelerate progress in scientific research and technological applications without major new investments, which are not likely to occur, is to break down some of these traditional barriers."[2] To this end, tax incentives, changes in patent law, and the instability of federal funding are all encouraging industrial support of academic research. Collaborative arrangements between industry and universities, however, carry new implications for proprietary controls.

Another factor complicating the matter of ownership and control of research findings is the public's demand for information, especially about controversial government policies or industrial practices. Growing public concern about the health effects of toxic wastes, environmental carcinogens, and chemicals in the workplace is reflected in state "right to know" legislation, in the increasing demands by citizens for research data, and in greater use of the Freedom of Information Act. Scientific findings are important in adversarial situations and in the litigation and public disputes that surround controversial technological decisions. The protagonists in technological disputes perceive the results of investigations as evidence to support their cause.[3] By demanding access to ongoing research, they also challenge the time-consuming process of validating investigations and peer review and therefore threaten the traditional expectations of scientists concerning their right to time the disclosure of their research findings.

Recently a trend toward increased government-imposed restrictions on the flow of information has emerged to counter the burden of public demands for information. Restrictions are taking the form of proposals to change the disclosure provisions of the Freedom of Information Act and to increase the number of exemptions to the act. National security and export controls are being tightened to limit the transfer of information out of the country. Research productivity is inevitably affected by these restrictive measures. Indeed, in a context where knowledge—its production and dissemination—is integrally linked with power and profit, scientists often find themselves embroiled in struggles over the control of the process of investigation, the data produced, and the ideas derived.

The pressures on researchers to produce results with the potential for commercial or military exploitation are transforming scientific data and even the research process into "intellectual property"—property which can be owned or possessed and is therefore subject to competing claims. Intellectual property is a legal term defined as "an aggregate of rights in the results of creative efforts of the mind"[4] and is usually used in reference to the intangible property rights involved in copyrights, trade secrets, or patents. In these domains, property is widely accepted as an appropriate concept. However, it is being applied more broadly to include the results of research, so that they too are subject to competing claims.

In extending the concept of property to research, the matter of professional control becomes a critical issue. Some degree of external control over the direction of science and the distribution of knowledge has long followed directly from the federal funding of research. Scientists who accept public funds assume a quasi-public status in that federal regulations require them to be accountable for the use of these funds, to meet certain obligations concerning ethical research methods, to give the sponsoring agency access to their results as stipulated in their funding agreement, and to accept certain obligations for public disclosure. The federal agency's choice of the instrument through which to support research—a grant, a contract, or a cooperative agreement—has practical importance for the recipient's control.[5] So too does the agency's concern about fiscal and managerial control over federally funded research. However, with the exception of classified military research, scientists have assumed that the data and concepts derived from projects funded by research grants, in contrast to contracts or cooperative agreements, essentially belong to the investigators, who may also decide when their work is ready for disclosure and what may be disclosed.

Scientists resist external control as a threat to the quality and integrity of research and as an infringement on their right to control the production and dissemination of their work. From this perspective, the question of ownership is unambiguous: the concept of individual sovereignty guides scientific behavior. The physicist Percy Bridgeman puts this bluntly:

> The process that I want to call scientific is a process that involves the continual apprehension of meaning, the constant appraisal of significance, accompanied by the running act of checking . . . . This checking and judging and accepting that together constitute understanding are done by me and can be done for me by no one else. They are as private as my toothache and without them science is doomed.[6]

In this context of individual sovereignty, the application of concepts of property to scientific ideas is extremely controversial. Although struggles over priority punctuate the history of science, scientists consider the claims as disputes within the community and an integral part of the process of research. Sociologist Robert Merton argues that, despite ubiquitous priority disputes, "property rights in science are whittled down to a bare minimum by the rationale of the scientific ethic. The scientist's claim to his intellectual 'property' is limited to that of recognition and esteem."[7]

Few principles exist which clarify the definition of intellectual property, whether in science or in other fields. In 1978, the House of Representatives Committee on Government Operations reported on the lack of guidelines for federal contracts and grant data. The report described the confused state of government policy concerning the disclosure of information as an "uncharted and undefined" area:

> There is no government information—or confidentiality—policy as such. Instead there is a profusion of inconsistent and often conflicting laws, policies, and practices which have developed over the years to suit specific program purposes or particular interest groups.[8]

Policies are especially confused with respect to the disclosure of scientific information. Legal standards governing policies for information disclosure cover only the Executive Branch or agency records. The standards are commonly extended to research records by analogy, but they often conflict with expectations about the autonomy of research. With few guiding principles, the struggle over control of scientific knowledge has taken the form of discrete disputes in which various parties stake their claims in terms of rights and responsibilities: the "right to know," the "right to privacy," the "right of access," the "right to control one's own product," the "obligation to protect research subjects," and the "responsibility to protect the public interest."

In the chapters that follow, I examine a number of the disputes that have centered on the control of or access to scientific information. The exchanges point up the diversity of situations in which questions of ownership are becoming important in science. The cases focus on how these disputes relate to secrecy in science and the freedom of scientists to control the disclosure of technical information and underscore the importance of consistency and responsibility in establishing principles of ownership and control.

Much of the discussion about intellectual property has come to focus on the commercialization of biomedical research. There are fears that the emergence of profitable new markets for scientific information will curtail the free exchange of ideas, or that the sponsorship of academic research by commercial interests will threaten traditional values guiding the practice of research. In quite a different and also widely debated area, scientists pursuing traditional kinds of research find themselves snared by changing information policies developed to protect the "leakage" of commercial or military technology to other nations. These issues are but part of a wider syndrome, and property disputes are taking place in many other arenas as well. Few of the issues of official secrecy, patenting, or military security are new; indeed, similar issues emerged with the burgeoning of the research enterprise after World War II. However, they are now assuming new proportions, challenging the norms traditionally governing scientific research, the structure of academic institutions, and the nature of research relationships. There is, in fact, much discussion these days about "renegotiating" the contract between science and society, and the efforts to resolve proprietary disputes are part of these negotiations.

The cases I examine are drawn from areas of research that have become a focus of proprietary disputes, and they were selected to illustrate contradictions in the policies and practices that currently govern the disclosure or protection of research information. The disputes fall into five identifiable categories:

- Some of the more visible disputes are occurring because proprietary interests in commercially competitive areas of research conflict with the principle of open communication in science.
- Some disputes occur because efforts to extend public access through the Freedom of Information Act to scientific data conflict with the scientists' desire to control the disclosure of their research.
- Some disputes take place because the right of public access conflicts with the researcher's obligation to protect the confidentiality of research sources or the privacy of research subjects.
- Questions of ownership and control arise when scientists attempt to disseminate health and safety data in what they believe to be the public's interest and are blocked by agencies or employers seeking to control the research they support.
- Finally, disputes take place when government extends national security restrictions to nonclassified research, obliterating traditions of free exchange of scientific knowledge and ideas as well as weakening distinctions between civilian and military research.

I have organized the chapters to highlight these categories of disputes, and in each area, have outlined the problems of negotiating consistent and acceptable policies for ownership and control of scientific information.[9]

2. Proprietary Secrecy Versus Open Communication in Science

In Los Angeles in 1977, a man with leukemia agreed to allow a sample of his blood-forming cells to be taken from his bone marrow for scientific research. The man died soon after his generous act. Claims over who may profit financially from his cells, however, have continued for years.

Two research hematologists at the University of California School of Medicine, Phillip Koeffler and David Golde, succeeded in making the man's cells grow and divide, producing a new cell line that could be used to study leukemia. The new cell line was called KG–1, and a sample was sent to Robert Gallo, of the National Cancer Institute, who was also interested in testing it. During a screening procedure, Gallo noticed that the cell line produced a low concentration of interferon, the body's natural antiviral protein. He then sent a sample of KG–1 to Sidney Pestka, a colleague who worked at the Roche Institute of Molecular Biology, an institution which is wholly funded by the pharmaceutical firm

Hoffman–La Roche. Pestka found that he could manipulate the cell cycle to make KG–1 an optimal medium for the production of interferon. Next, at Genentech, a biotechnology firm with contracts from Hoffman–La Roche, a technique was devised whereby substantial quantities of interferon genes could be manufactured from the KG–1. Because of the potential for an enormously profitable enterprise, a major dispute ensued between the University of California and Hoffman–La Roche over who in fact owned the KG–1 interferon gene.[1] The university, as the home of the scientists who had created the cell line, claimed ownership and the right to royalties from the production of interferon. Hoffman–La Roche also claimed ownership; in fact, the drug firm filed a patent application covering both the interferon and the manufacturing process. Lawyers for the university viewed the drug firm as making unauthorized use of material developed by university researchers and accused Hoffman–La Roche of seeking to profit from the open exchange of information and material among academic scientists. The dispute continued until January 1983, when it was settled out of court: the drug company retained the right to use the interferon gene and KG–1 cells, but paid an undisclosed sum to the university, thereby recognizing its property rights.

Priority disputes are hardly unusual in the scientific community. Research is a competitive enterprise, and prestige and recognition come to those who publish first. But now, with the potential for high profits from research in fields such as molecular biology, claims and challenges to claims of ownership of research results are more and more common.

In the fall of 1980, such a priority dispute expanded into a battle over patent rights potentially worth millions of dollars.[2] A team of researchers from the University of California, San Diego (UCSD), and the Salk Institute at La Jolla, California, submitted a manuscript to the National Academy of Sciences that described in essence a new research method for identifying proteins immunologically by creating synthetic antigens. Because these synthetic antigens could stimulate the production of antibodies to various proteins or viruses, they might serve as the basis for inexpensive, safe, and easily available synthetic vaccines. Five days after the UCSD-Salk group submitted their paper, a research team from the Scripps Clinic and Research Foundation, also in La Jolla, submitted a manuscript to *Nature* that described essentially the same method. According to UCSD scientist Russell Doolittle, the Scripps team should have acknowledged the work shared by UCSD on the method. However, Richard Lerner, head of the Scripps group, said that he thought of the method independently. Initially, when the issue was simply publication, the UCSD team was inclined to ignore its claim to the method. But when the Scripps team filed a patent application for the procedure and negotiated a joint venture with the medical supply company Johnson & Johnson to produce vaccines, the possibility of considerable profit was at stake.

Whatever the outcome of the claims, one thing is clear to Doolittle: "There used to be a good, healthy exchange of ideas and information among researchers at UCSD, the Salk Institute, and the Scripps Clinic. Now we are locking our doors."[3]

Disputes such as the two just described suggest how the competitive situation created by the commercialization of molecular biology may be eroding the pattern of open communication and exchange of information essential in this field, and in others as well. Stanford University

President Donald Kennedy noted that ominous changes in the pattern of scientific interchanges were already occurring in the 1970s: "Scientists who once shared prepublication information freely and exchanged cell lines without hesitation are now much more reluctant to do so. . . . The fragile network of informal communication that characterizes every especially active field is liable to rupture."[4]

The implications of disrupting traditional norms of scientific communication are far-reaching. As Harvard Professor of Science Policy Harvey Brooks warned: "The overemphasis on proprietary information and competition may inhibit the development of a field which has hitherto benefitted from open and rapid exchange of information and data on a worldwide basis."[5] Questions arise as to whether the mutual trust that has allowed informal patterns of scientific communication will obtain in new research areas when the potential for commercialization promises profit as well as prestige for scientific discovery, or whether unwritten codes of ethics that guide scientific behavior will be viable in the current economic context.

Several related developments have exacerbated concerns about competition-induced secrecy in science, including critical changes in patent policy pertaining to university research and the commercial possibilities inherent in certain areas of basic science. Together with the declining federal support for university training and research, these developments have encouraged new contractual arrangements bearing on ownership and control.

Patenting Research

The patent system provides incentives for invention

by granting exclusive property rights for technological innovations. This system, created by the Patent Act of 1793, reflected Thomas Jefferson's insight that "ingenuity should receive a liberal encouragement." Later, Lincoln described its purpose as "adding the fuel of interest to the fire of genius." It was in this spirit of fueling research that Chief Justice Warren E. Burger of the U.S. Supreme Court approved the patent application of a General Electric Company molecular biologist for a method of producing a genetically engineered bacterium that is capable of breaking down crude oil. The court, in a five to four decision, held that "a live human-made microorganism is patentable subject matter,"[6] but declined to comment on the moral arguments raised about "the gruesome parade of horribles" that might emerge from such research.

Soon after the Supreme Court decision, Herbert Boyer of the University of California, San Francisco, and Stanley Cohen of Stanford patented a process for inserting foreign genetic material into a bacterial plasmid, a technique widely used in recombinant DNA research. Boyer and Cohen assigned their patent rights to their institutions, which charge users a fee for a license to use the technique. Since the 1980 Supreme Court decision, patent applications involving the creation of new microorganisms and gene-splicing methods have proliferated.

The court decision came at a time when the Congress was also reevaluating patent policy, in an effort to provide greater incentives for research and technological innovation. Before 1980, patent policy with respect to government-supported research was in a state of confusion. Twenty-six different patent policies were in effect as each government agency developed its own rules. For example, the Department of Energy required grantees to submit papers to the agency for prior patent review 60 days before submitting them for publication in the professional journals. In the case of research funded by the Department of Health, Education, and Welfare, patent rights reverted to the department. But the government has not been efficient in turning its thousands of patents to profit: only about 4 percent of some 30,000 government-owned patents have been marketed.[7] Furthermore, the government policy of granting nonexclusive licenses discourages investment; lacking an exclusive license, a company is reluctant to pay the cost of developing a product, and potentially valuable research has remained unexploited.

It was the growing concern about the so-called innovation lag that prompted congressional efforts to develop a uniform patent policy that would encourage commercial development of government-funded research. The Patent and Trademark Amendment Act (Public Law 96–517), which was passed on 12 December 1980, allows universities, small business firms, and nonprofit institutions to apply for patents on federally funded research and to retain exclusive licenses for their patents for up to eight years. The government is entitled to a royalty-free license; royalties are to be shared with the inventor and the profits used to support further research.[8]

This law, which went into effect in July 1981, is similar—except for a clause in the implementation guidelines—to the patent agreement policy of the National Institutes of Health (NIH). The guidelines for the law's implementation contain two controversial clauses. First, the government maintains "march-in rights"—that is, the right to intervene if a discovery is not properly marketed within a reasonable period of time. Second, and more critical, funding agencies can require that the government be informed about patentable research three months before any results are submitted for publication or disclosed at a professional society meeting. Failure to meet this deadline can result in the forfeit of the patent.

The Office of Management and Budget (OMB), which developed the guidelines, insisted on the second clause in order to protect patent rights overseas. In the United States, an investigator who presents work at a symposium or in a publication has up to twelve months to apply for a patent, but some European countries consider submission of a manuscript as an act of public disclosure that would jeopardize the validity of a patent. Viewing the OMB restriction as unrealistic in the university research context, NIH decided to drop the notification clause from its rules.

When the principles of patent law are applied to research results, certain problems inherent in that law are transferred as well. Economist Joan Robinson described well the paradox inherent in the patent law:

> A patent is a device to prevent the diffusion of new methods before the original investor has recovered profit adequate to induce the requisite investment. The justification of the patent system is that by slowing down the diffusion of technical progress it ensures that there will be more progress to diffuse. . . . Since it is rooted in a contradiction, there can be no such thing as an ideally beneficial patent system, and it is bound to produce negative results in particular instances, impeding progress unnecessarily even if its general effect is favorable on balance.[9]

The late Arthur Bueche, vice president for research at General Electric, put the issue succinctly in terms of industrial interests: "If we could not maintain secrecy, research would be of little value. Research properly leads to patents that protect ideas, but were it not for secrecy, it would be difficult to create a favorable patent position."[10]

Although patents are intended to avert proprietary secrecy, there are conflicting views about the appropriateness of patenting and the actual effects on secrecy. Once an invention is licensed, the patent provides the exclusive right to commercial exploitation, and proprietary secrecy is no longer needed. However, the system may also inhibit open discussions and communication of results during early stages of research. Thus, the patent process, which encourages disclosure and dissemination of information once a patent is sought, may actually promote secrecy in the interest of patent priority.[11] Researchers may, for example, be reluctant to report on their work at meetings or may delay publication until a patent application is filed. "Patent first, publish later," is a slogan widely heard as collaborative arrangements between private industry and academia multiply.

Biocommerce

The cooperation between industries and universities that began in the early part of the century played a major role in shaping the educational system and the direction of scientific research in academia.[12] However, the role of personnel, and the proprietary distinctions, were until recently relatively well defined. Applied research in chemistry, for example, was conducted mainly in industrial research laboratories, quite apart from the universities which supplied the research personnel. Scientists often had to choose between autonomous work in poorly equipped university laboratories or highly directed research in better-funded industrial laboratories.

This increased industry-university collaboration in the early part of the century was driven—much as it is today—by foreign competition. Collaboration served both partners well. It was a means both to expand the limited resources of universities and to meet the long-run needs of industrial firms. In 1905, for example, William Walker established, with industrial funds, the applied chemistry laboratory at the Massachusetts Institute of Technology (MIT), declaring that "the distinction which has existed between the terms pure science and applied science is falling away."[13] In 1913, the American Association for the Advancement of Science formed the Committee of 100 to promote industry-university cooperation, and one of its early tasks was to prepare an inventory of researchers and their projects.

Over the next few decades industry provided resources to universities for training and research in exchange for technically trained manpower and scientific expertise. The programs developed included an industrial fellowship system at the University of Kansas, a technology plan at MIT, and the Mellon program at the University of Pittsburgh. When industrial support waned during the depression of the 1930s, universities began to look for more stable sources of support. This came through the increase in federal funding of research, especially after World War II. In the area of biology, the Public Health Service Act of 1944 provided legislative authority for the granting of government research funds to universities. Subsequently, NIH assumed responsibility for basic research in biology and medicine, and the National Science Foundation (NSF) did so in other fields.[14]

Industrial relationships continued but were limited mainly to individual consulting (fee-for-service) arrangements, scholarship programs, or contracts to specific groups, mostly in engineering schools. There were some partnerships on specific projects and cooperative programs in which industrial associations had access to academic work, but usually only for procured services and in exchange for a fee. These joint ventures seldom applied to basic research, which was considered to be a very marginal investment unlikely to yield immediate return.

Industrial funding remained at a relatively low level and made up only 3.8 percent of the total university research budget in 1980. Seldom controversial, it provided contacts and financial benefits usually only to individual faculty members, and on the whole it did not divert them from university responsibilities. Agreements, usually negotiated individually, were generally small in scale, and questions of proprietary interest were decided with relative ease.

The situation began to change in the mid-1970s. Universities began to experience economic pressures from declining student enrollments, rising operating costs, and a pattern of federal research and training support that failed to keep pace with the expanding academic community of scientists. At the same time, federal grant and contract regulations were imposing increasing burdens on both researchers and administrators. Economic and bureaucratic pressures have left many faculty and university administrators receptive to, indeed, eager for industrial support, and inevitably less critical of the implications for the ownership and control of research. To many institutions, private-sector investment appears as a means to renew vitality and to find more stable support in a less regulated environment.

Government officials and advisers, concerned about

the competitiveness of the United States in high-technology areas that depend on basic research, have also encouraged private investment. In October 1979, a Department of Commerce advisory committee on industrial innovation noted that this "key national source of new technical knowledge is not being adequately tapped for its innovative potentiality by the private sector."[15] The National Commission on Research also recommended expanding industry-university cooperation in research and development.[16]

Responding to these recommendations, Congress passed the Stevenson-Wydler Technology Innovation Act (Public Law 96–480) in 1980, providing the statutory framework for establishing industrial-technology centers at universities. These centers are financed jointly by the federal government and industry, but the government's share must be gradually reduced over time. Bills proposed in both the Senate and the House of Representatives to provide tax credits for industrial investments in university research and development in biogenetics, microelectronics, and some areas of energy research have so far been unsuccessful.

One change is affecting largely biogenetic research, where the traditional fee-for-service consulting arrangements made by individual scientists are turning into equity participation in new venture-capital firms. Universities, too, are looking at new institutional arrangements that will bring them into closer collaboration with commercial ventures.

The rapidly changing viewpoints about individual entrepreneurial ventures in science are illustrated by the case of microbiologist Leonard Hayflick.[17] In 1976, Hayflick, then at Stanford University, was embroiled in a conflict with NIH over the ownership of a cell line that he had developed in the 1960s. It was the first strain of normal human cells that could be established in a culture, and he formed a company to market the cells which were found to be useful in the production of vaccines. NIH publicly charged Hayflick with profiting from research conducted with federal support and claimed that the cells belonged to the government. Stanford was apparently about to take disciplinary action when Hayflick resigned. He filed suit seeking title to the cells and the proceeds from sales. After a long, often acrimonious dispute, the case was settled out of court in 1981, with Hayflick retaining the money from sales but with the question of ownership of the cell line still unresolved.

Today Hayflick's actions would not be controversial. It is now accepted practice for scientists and institutions to profit directly from the results of academic research through various types of commercial ventures. Several hundred new firms have sprouted in the field of biotechnology, for example, since the first, Cetus Corporation, was formed in 1975.

Investors, anticipating the commercial potential, place high value on the research process itself. The market for industrial applications of genetic research is estimated at $40 billion over the next few decades.[18] Such research is expected to yield improved crops with increased resistance to disease or reduced fertilizer needs. It is expected to produce medical products such as human insulin, interferon, growth hormones, vaccines, and commercial products such as industrial enzymes and food additives. The chemical, mining, and energy industries also look forward to long-term benefits from genetic research—for the recovery and leaching of minerals, the recovery of oil, and pollution control.[19] The value of the research will ultimately depend on the ability to use genetically engineered microbes more efficiently than existing techniques permit. In the meantime, it is clear that the research itself is "valuable intellectual property . . . that may eventually be turned into useful and profitable products."[20]

Universities are already involved in a variety of agreements to augment research funds.[21] In 1974, for example, Monsanto agreed to pay about $25 million to the Harvard Medical School for a twelve-year research project on a tumor-blocking agent. The company has also supplied cultures to the school and has provided some money to endow a professorship. In return, the contract calls for Harvard researchers to exchange information with Monsanto staff. Each party can patent its own inventions, but Monsanto has exclusive licensing rights.

In 1980, Harvard, through Massachusetts General Hospital, accepted $50 million, to be provided over ten years, from the German pharmaceutical firm Hoechst to establish a research department in genetic engineering. The collaboration is to be overseen by a board consisting of three representatives from the hospital and three from Hoechst; the latter retains exclusive rights worldwide to license new developments. The arrangement has raised questions about whether research conducted at the hospital over many years with federal funds would now be exploited by a foreign firm. In addition, because Massachusetts General Hospital still receives about $30 million a year in NIH research funds, there were questions of whether the Hoechst agreement would violate the Patent and Trademarks Amendment Act if some of the NIH funds were involved in the new venture.[22] A General Accounting Office investigation, however, found that no federal funds would be used to support the new laboratory and that legal precedent indicates that government funding of research that serves as a building block for later work is not sufficient grounds to claim a patent infringement.[23]

The largest joint venture to date is an institute for research in biology directly tied to MIT and financed by Edwin Whitehead, chairman of a medical instrumentation company.[24] He has provided $20 million to build the institution, $7.5 million in general purpose funds, and $5 million a year to operate the institute. The institute will also receive an endowment of $100 million when Whitehead dies. Patent rights are held by the new institute and reinvested to finance further research, but MIT shares royalties on an equal basis. Although administered separately from MIT (by a board of directors that includes Whitehead's children), institute researchers are full faculty members at the university. The new institute benefits from the affiliation with a prestigious university, and the university gains twenty additional research staff, with two endowments for professorships. However, MIT may lose control over the recruitment of a staff that could eventually comprise about a third of the biology department. The plan, however cautiously negotiated, has raised a storm of protest. As one professor saw it, "Mr. Whitehead proposes to buy a piece of MIT."[25] Facing a deficit of $2.5 million, the MIT administration chose to accept the money for new programs that it could not otherwise pursue.

Similar centers are being created at other major research universities. Stanford and the University of California at Berkeley, for example, have formed a Center for Biotechnology Research with funds from six chemical, engineering, and biotechnology companies. Cornell has formed a Biotechnology Institute to attract funds from diverse industrial sources.

These agreements are limited partnerships in which private investors join forces with university research centers and hope for a return on their investment in research. Michigan State University has taken a further step and formed a company, Neogen, to exploit the commercial potential of its biotechnology research. Neogen is set up as a corporation to attract venture capital and to develop and market innovations arising out of university research. In 1980, the Harvard University administration considered a plan to form its own genetic engineering firm to license, produce, and even market results of research. There was so much opposition from faculty, who envisioned conflicts between commercial interests and academic values, that Harvard eventually rejected the plan.[26]

By the end of 1981, however, contracts had been signed or were in the final stages of negotiations at eight institutions for major new departments or research centers to be funded by industrial sources at a total cost of over $200 million. Moreover, industrial support of academic research is generally increasing. According to Nelson Schneider of DNA Research, a biotechnology firm formed by E. F. Hutton, the private sector is rapidly increasing its share of biomedical research support in academic centers, as shown in the statistics that he presented to Congress (Table 1).

Negotiations
Collaborative arrangements between industry and universities are a means to finance new research programs and also to bring the results of research to the marketplace. The structure of these arrangements with respect to patent and licensing agreements is a major point

Table 1. Funding for biomedical research in academic centers.

Year	Funding		
	NIH (in billions)	Private sector (in millions)	Ratio (NIH: private)
1979	$1.9	$100	19:1
1980	$2.1	$150 to 200	10:1
1981 (est.)	$2.28	$400 to 500	5:1

Source: Nelson M. Schneider, Testimony at Hearings on Commercialization of Academic Biomedical Research, U.S. House of Representatives, Subcommittees on Science, Research and Technology and Investigations and Oversight, 97th Congress, June 8, 1981, Washington: USGPO, 1981, p. 127.

of negotiation. Universities prefer to retain ownership of patents, offering exclusive marketing licenses to the industry supporting the research. Corporate sponsors of research usually prefer to hold the patent rights themselves, and, in fact, would often prefer trade secrecy arrangements. The latter is especially true in fields where patents rapidly become obsolete and litigation might limit their value as a source of protection. The nature of the developing university-industry agreements varies widely, often depending not so much on the needs of the negotiating parties as on their bargaining strength. Contracts are clearly a matter of price as well as of ethics.

Even carefully structured arrangements may raise sensitive proprietary issues that concern not only the parties involved in the negotiations but, in a sense, the public as well. For instance, the research investments of the private sector may be made at a late stage in the research process, after a long period of public investment to build knowledge and competency in the field. It would be possible in such a case that, on the basis of a relatively modest investment, a private-sector firm could reap profits well beyond the scope of its investment. This issue surfaced in the case of the Hoechst-Massachusetts General Hospital contract. The question of government ownership is also complicated when government and industry are supporting the same research, a situation referred to as the "comingling" of research funds.[27] Accounting systems that could sort out such mixed investments are not likely to work well when applied to the generation of ideas.

Conflicts of interest are also bound to arise in situations in which university faculty are directly involved in commercial ventures. The academic responsibility of open communication inevitably conflicts with the commercial responsibility to maintain proprietary secrecy. Donald Kennedy has described incidents at scientific meetings in which scientists refuse to divulge details of a technique because they consider them to be proprietary information.[28]

Secrecy in research precludes replication and weakens the system of peer review. It may also cause conflicts for graduate students, postdoctoral researchers, and younger faculty who need to further their academic careers through publication. Beyond the problems of secrecy, conflicts over the actual control of the direction and details of research supported by private-sector investment are inevitable. And faculty who maintain a dual role as academic scholars and entrepreneurs face conflicting goals in their relationships with students and colleagues. Indeed, graduate students at some universities have complained that their research options are limited as they are diverted to those areas of commercial potential of interest to their advisors.

In his 1980 report to the university overseers, Harvard President Derek Bok summarized the implications of the new relationships between industry and the academy: on the positive side are opportunities to generate new sources of income that could contribute to maintaining the quality of research by providing fellowships and funds for recruiting new staff, upgrading equipment, and generating new lines of inquiry; on the negative side are conflicts with a university's commitment to the extension and dissemination of knowledge.[29] If ties to industry encourage secrecy, divert faculty away from university-centered research and education, bring external control over the direction of research, and allow profit motives to enter decisions about hiring or promotion, then such ties may indeed erode what is left of the image of the university as a detached institution able to provide relatively impartial, independent, and therefore credible expertise.[30]

It is not the first time that concerns about independence have distressed scientists and university presidents. In the 1930s the move toward federally supported research provoked similar worries, and the National Academy of Sciences objected in principle to having private universities accept government funds.[31] In 1934, MIT President Karl T. Compton, who also headed the Science Advisory Board to President Franklin D. Roosevelt, wrote the following:

> I must confess to considerable doubt as to the wisdom of advocating federal support of scien-

tific research . . . . If government financial support should carry with it government control of
research programs or research workers . . . any
consideration should dictate the administration
of funds other than the inherent worth of a
project or the capabilities of a scientist, or if the
funds should fluctuate considerably in amount
with the political fortunes of an administration
or the varying ideas of Congress, then government support would probably do more harm
than good. . . .[32]

Clearly, fears about the integrity of research are not
new to the country, but the norms that have governed
proprietary rights in science are now often found to be
inadequate. Accordingly, the character of university-industry research relationships, and in particular the many
problems associated with biocommerce, are the focus of
studies by, for example, the General Accounting Office,
the National Academy of Sciences, the Office of Technology Assessment, the National Commission on Research, and universities themselves. Although mostly
inconclusive, the studies do propose guidelines appropriate to the present social and economic context of basic
research.

University administrators are considering ways to
specify formally faculty obligations once considered a
matter of individual responsibility and trust. One proposal, for example, would have patent rights and responsibilities spelled out at the time a faculty member is
hired. Another would require disclosure of all consulting
arrangements and any relationships with private firms.
Still another would set down explicit guidelines for consulting and entrepreneurial ventures.[33] A Harvard Uni-

versity committee on extramural activities issued guidelines for faculty activities stating, among other things, that a professor cannot be an operating officer of a commercial concern. At the University of California a special task force is examining the question of proprietary rights. Different policies are emerging on the confidentiality of contracts: Stanford requires full disclosure; Harvard allows confidential contract agreements.

Faced with the novel situation of scientists who themselves are commercializing their research, most university administrators are proceeding with caution in formalizing controls. Draconian restrictions could prompt the departure of some of the more active and creative faculty, sapping the vitality of academic departments. It is expected that when the commercial potential of biogenetic research becomes a reality, more research scientists will make a choice between academic or business careers. At least one scientist, biochemist Walter Gilbert, a Nobel Laureate and president of Biogen, has made his choice—he resigned his Harvard professorship.

Stanford's Donald Kennedy has proposed that a second Asilomar conference be convened to debate the hazards of potential profits and the question of proprietary control. (The subject of the first Asilomar conference in 1976 was potential hazards from recombinant DNA research). In 1982 he brought together the presidents of five research universities and directors of eleven corporations at Pajaro Dunes, California, to discuss the areas of consensus and potential conflict in the emerging industry-university relationships. To avoid the inhibitions of publicity, the discussion was closed to the public and the press. Although agreeing that collaboration is of benefit and that arrangements must preserve basic academic values, the participants apparently could not agree on how to implement these general principles. Questions about the disclosure of contract arrangements, the granting of exclusive licenses, and the ways to deal with conflicts of interest were not resolved.

Federal agencies have, however, already initiated proposals to deal with their proprietary concerns. NIH has recommended that all institutions receiving funds have a written patent policy. In June 1980, the NIH Recombinant DNA Advisory Committee, concerned about the possibility of disclosure of trade secrets during the review process, revised its guidelines to provide for the protection of proprietary information at this stage. Only members of the advisory committee and its staff would have access to the proposals, and all are required to sign a document affirming their adherence to the guidelines governing confidentiality of proprietary information. They must also keep all material in locked files. A NIH working group recommended that its study sections adopt similar procedures.

Faced with unstable federal research support and burgeoning paperwork, academic scientists are accepting industrial liaisons that may dramatically change their traditional role. Academic science has been a public resource, a repository for ideas, and a source of relatively unbiased information. Industrial connections blur the distinctions between corporations and the university, establishing private control over a public resource. Problems of secrecy and proprietary rights are inherent in these new relationships and hold serious implications for both academic science and the public interest. Those involved in negotiating these relationships see the problems that are now so evident in biomedical research as but a harbinger of things to come:

> Others will soon be facing the same maze of issues: intellectual property rights; the need for support of scholarly work; questions of the impact of proprietary controls; and the proper role of the university in entrepreneurial efforts. These issues will appear not only in the area of biomedicine, but in other parts of science as well.[34]

3. Public Access Versus Professional Control

In 1976, a group of physicians filed a request under the Freedom of Information Act (FOIA) for data gathered during a long-term clinical study of the effects of five diabetes treatment regimens in which 1000 diabetes patients were monitored for periods ranging from five to eight years. A private consortium of twelve medical centers called the University Group Diabetes Program (UGDP) had conducted the study with a $15-million grant from the National Institute for Arthritis, Metabolism, and Digestive Diseases of the National Institutes of Health (NIH). Although NIH had the right of access to the raw data, the agency never exercised its right.

The UGDP researchers found that certain drug regimens might increase the incidence of heart disease among diabetes patients without any offsetting benefits. They reported their early findings at the 1970 meeting of the American Diabetes Association and published them in the December 1970 issue of the association's journal.[1] The findings generated considerable controversy because of their potential influence on the fate of the drug in question. Although the extent of influence of the studies is not clear, the Food and Drug Administration (FDA) proposed changes in the labeling requirements for certain drugs used in the treatment of diabetes after learning of the UGDP study. Then, on the basis of the UGDP findings, the Secretary of Health, Education, and Welfare (HEW) defined one drug as an "imminent hazard" and suspended the FDA procedure for approving the medication for clinical use. An administrative law judge confirmed the suspension order. Later, in 1978, the FDA ordered the drug withdrawn from the market. The influence on policy of the UGDP study was used by a national association of physicians, called the Committee on the Care of the Diabetic, to justify their request, under the FOIA, for the UGDP data. This group was concerned that a useful therapeutic tool was being removed unnecessarily from the market. When UGDP denied them access to the data on the grounds that research was still underway, the physicians brought suit.[2] They argued that since the study was federally funded and was used in making administrative decisions, the data were "agency records," subject to the terms of the FOIA.

In 1978, the U.S. Court of Appeals ruled that the data, which were not actually in the possession of the NIH, did not constitute agency records.[3] This decision rested on statutory language defining an agency record as material that an agency has "created or obtained." Noting that federal funding through a research grant does not by itself define research as an agency record and that the "public interest" concerns of the plaintiffs were not relevant, Judge Harold Leventhal did not require disclosure. He commented on the "stupendous" quantity of documents involved in research and the "awesome" implications of disclosure requirements. And he drew distinctions between an audit of documents filed with the federal government and "an agreement to accept rummaging by the world at large."[4]

In a dissenting opinion, Judge David Bazelon argued that federal funding of the research and reliance on the data from regulatory action were sufficient grounds to require public disclosure. The FOIA, after all, was created on the premise that the public has a right to know what the government is doing. Thus, Bazelon wrote, it follows that data underlying government actions must be open to public scrutiny.[5] However, in 1980, Justice Brennan of the Supreme Court, upholding the lower court decisions, said:

> Federal participation in the generation of the data by means of a grant from HEW does not make the private organization a federal "agency" within the terms of the Act. Nor does this federal funding . . . render the data "agency records" of HEW . . . .[6]

A case with a different outcome also focused on the issue of possession of data.[7] In 1978, Milo Shannon-Thornberry completed data collection for a study of the socioeconomic factors affecting infant feeding practices and the relative effect of bottle and breast feeding on morbidity and mortality rates. A group of nonprofit, church-related organizations, including the National Council of Churches, had funded the research. Lacking the computer facilities to compile and analyze the data, Thornberry enlisted the help of the Centers for Disease Control (CDC) in tabulating the data. He agreed in return to make the survey data available to the agency. In April 1979, CDC announced its participation in the study. It decided, however, to limit its involvement to the actual computer work and to avoid any data analysis.

The following September, two manufacturers of infant formula, Mead-Johnson and Abbott Laboratories, requested the raw data from the CDC, invoking the FOIA to justify their right to claim data held by a federal agency. Thornberry and his sponsors objected: they had collected the data with private financing long before CDC was involved and had spent an estimated 6040 hours creating and implementing the survey. CDC's work, estimated at 496 hours, was of a mechanical and clerical nature. The association with CDC had developed on the assumption that no data would be released until the investigators themselves had analyzed and published the results. Thornberry also feared that the intent of the request would be to subvert findings threatening to corporate interests.

In its April 1980 decision, the U.S. District Court in Atlanta, Georgia, held that CDC's possession of the data and its involvement in the project defined the data as "agency records."[8] Unlike the situation in the UGDP case, in which there had been federal funding but no agency involvement, the requested computer tapes were actually created with direct agency participation. Thus, the court considered disclosure under the FOIA, even prior to analysis, as appropriate, but it avoided the issue the researchers raised concerning the purpose of the FOIA request. In fact, the intent in obtaining the data promptly became apparent when Ross Laboratories, a division of Abbott, circulated a letter to doctors questioning the credibility of the research.

In these two cases the requests were for data from completed studies, one funded by the government, the other by private sources. The nature of the public interest in disclosure differed in the two cases. In the UGDP case, some of the data from the diabetes study had been published, and a group of physicians sought access to data in order to verify findings that might have implications for clinical practice. In the Thornberry case, a group with commercial interests demanded access, and the scientist, who had disclosed data to a public agency, resisted further disclosure. In both cases, the requests infringed on the scientists' desire to protect their data until they could complete their analyses and publish their results. They were operating within the normal academic expectation that the scientists who generate the data have proprietary rights to that data. Moreover, they questioned the intent of the requests, suggesting that the public interest would be better served by withholding disclosure until the data were fully analyzed. In neither case, however, did the decision address issues about the implications of disclosure for the public interest, issues which derive more from the intent of the FOIA requests and the potential policy use of the research than from the procedural point of possession.

Requests for data from long-term clinical, epidemiological, and toxicological studies present similar problems for scientists. One such case involved a demand for data from an ongoing toxicological study at the University of Wisconsin in which the effect on Rhesus monkeys of dioxin isomer TCDD used in the herbicide 2,4,5-T (2,4,5-trichlorophenoxyacetic acid) was under investigation.[9] Dow Chemical Company tried to obtain data from the federally funded study through an administrative subpoena served by the Environmental Protection Agency (EPA). Although not an FOIA case, the dispute reveals another side of the conflict inherent in the public's right of access and the researcher's right of professional control.

As detailed in the court records, in 1979, James Allen, a researcher at the University of Wisconsin, described preliminary results from one part of his dioxin study in testimony at an EPA public hearing. The EPA was considering whether to extend the temporary emergency ban on the use of dioxin in commercial pesticides. After the hearing, Dow requested Allen's data on the grounds that once research results are made public, the data must be available for cross-examination.

When an EPA administrative law judge granted Dow's request and issued a subpoena for the data, Allen, backed by the University of Wisconsin, refused to comply. They argued that the work was neither complete nor properly analyzed and that the testimony was only a preliminary progress report—part of a larger project involving studies not yet subject to the scrutiny of the scientific community through peer review. Moreover, they said that the subpoenaed documents contained other data not ready for disclosure and that extracting the requested material would be expensive. And finally, they argued that disclosure of data at this point might preclude scientific publication at a cost to both the scientists and the people who should ultimately benefit from the research.

Allen's conviction for misuse of federal funds to pay for a ski vacation and his subsequent resignation from the university complicated the issue by casting doubt on his credibility. However, representatives of the university continued to resist Dow's demands on the grounds that scientists themselves had the right, under the First Amendment's protection of freedom of expression, to judge the timing of disclosure and that intrusion by outsiders must be avoided. Following this argument, a U.S. District Court judge overturned the subpoena.[10]

Judge Barbara Crabb indicated that disclosure of data to a company with obvious vested interests could jeopardize a costly study prior to its completion and that the public interest was better served by withholding data until after peer review. The judge also argued for the importance of scientific autonomy in determining the timing of disclosure. Then, in February 1982, the U.S. Court of Appeals upheld the decision, placing considerable emphasis on the relation of scientific autonomy to academic freedom: "Intrusions into the enterprise of university research . . . are capable of chilling the exercise of academic freedom.[11] However, Judge Pell, who wrote a concurring decision, raised question about the obligations of public disclosure inherent in public funding of research and thus took issue with the idea that academic freedom automatically overrides the importance of public disclosure.[12] However, it is precisely this idea, resting on assumptions about the importance of scientific autonomy, that pervades the persistent disputes over access under the Freedom of Information Act.

Freedom of Information and Research

The President signed the FOIA into law in 1966. The act evolved from the assumption, fundamental to democratic ideology, that government accountability rests on an informed citizenry.[13] It was revised and extended in 1974 during a period of wide public concern about information disclosure for purposes of consumer and environmental protection. The revisions reflected an effort to prevent deceptive practices, to facilitate comparison of consumer products, to warn the public of hazards, and above all to open government decision-making to public review. Consistent with these goals, the FOIA requires that the public have access to all government agency records except for specified exempted material such as trade secrets, financial data, national defense information, and personnel or medical records whose disclosure would constitute an invasion of privacy. Scientists sought to have research included under the trade secrecy exemption, arguing that data are the scientists' "stock in trade"; however, until a reform bill proposed in 1981, which specifically includes research along with trade secrets, application of the FOIA to science has been oblique. Language included in this reform bill (S. 1730) would have made the trade secrets exemption applicable to the noncommercial research of scientists, but this bill was not enacted before the adjournment of the 97th Congress.

The scientific community is confronted with many FOIA requests for research proposals and for data from ongoing research projects funded by federal agencies. Requests to the NIH, for example, increased from 300 in 1975 to 1638 in 1979.[14] At one time the sheer quantity of data gathered in a research project automatically limited such demands, but with today's computer technology this is no longer an effective constraint. The request for the data in the diabetes treatment study, for example, was not considered impractical although there were an estimated 55 million documents pertaining to 1000 patients. If such demands become more frequent, the traditional expectations of scientists regarding their proprietary rights will be increasingly contested.

Research proposals may contain theoretical analyses, detailed bibliographies, research plans, and preliminary data from research in progress that often represent significant groundwork for an investigation. Scientists may hesitate to share such material, since disclosure might threaten the integrity of the evaluation process based on peer review, jeopardize potential patent rights, or allow plagiarism or pirating of ideas. They point out that requests for disclosure often come from individuals or firms seeking information that could serve their special interests in a competitive economic environment.[15]

Scientists are especially concerned with controlling the timing of disclosure of data from long-term studies.[16] Much attention has been given to protecting data from clinical trials, which are costly, long-term prospective studies designed to assess the value of diagnostic and therapeutic health care devices, practices, or treatments. Ideally, the participants in such trials are randomly assigned to experimental and control groups, and neither the subject nor the investigator knows which treatment the subject receives for the duration of the trial. Maintaining uncertainty about the results of treatment over a long period is basic to this research method. Premature disclosure of treatments or early findings could jeopardize the validity of the project and bias future results.

Questions of disclosure in clinical trials arise mostly when preliminary data reveal trends that indicate either the superiority of one treatment or possible unanticipated harm from a treatment to the research subjects. Should emerging trends that have not yet reached a level of statistical significance be disclosed? Are the measures of statistical significance acceptable to the scientific community adequate in cases where emerging trends indicate potential harm? Disclosure would certainly disrupt and often terminate the clinical trial, precluding definite data on the safety and efficacy of a new treatment. But failure to disclose emerging trends could be ethically dubious, depending on the magnitude of the threat and the significance of the emerging trends.[17] The possibility of disclosure might force physicians conducting clinical trials to reevaluate the consequences of their research more often. If, for example, the infamous Tuskegee syphilis study, a classic abuse of human subjects research, had been open to public scrutiny, the behavior of the scientists who knowingly used a group of syphilitics as controls when treatment was available might have been different.[18]

Clinical trials are an important part of the NIH budget. In 1978, the agency had in process 845 active clinical trials at a cost of about $150 million. An individual trial may cost more than $50 million total and take 10 years to complete. Responsibility for this research rests with the investigators who are accountable to an Institutional Review Board and to a Data and Safety Monitoring Committee.

Although FOIA requests for data from clinical trials are rare—according to NIH, only one has been made to date—the possibility of such requests provoked NIH to consider protective measures. The data from clinical trials have economic importance to manufacturers of drugs and medical products, physicians, and other researchers. Because the FOIA does not allow a federal agency to withhold data considered to be agency records, NIH requires grantees to keep all research records; the agency keeps only the summaries and results of analyses. In addition, the NIH director has sought statutory protection for data from clinical trials.

Negotiations

During the dispute between Dow Chemical and University of Wisconsin investigator James Allen, the university administrators sought legal grounds to resist the disclosure of raw research data from ongoing research. They found themselves in "an unexplored area of the law."[19] They appealed to well-known scientists and found wide support for the position that investigators and their referees are solely responsible for deciding when to disseminate their work. In a a letter to the assistant attorney general of Wisconsin in support of Allen's case, John Edsall, Harvard University chemist and former chairman of the AAAS Committee on Scientific Freedom and Responsibility, wrote, "When outsiders demand access to such records before the findings are published . . . they are in effect appropriating valuable property of the scientists who have done the research."[20] The court later concurred, protecting the autonomy of the scientist and his control over research.

Scientists are attacking the problem of how to define the terms of public access to research in several ways. Their negotiations include efforts to bring research under the trade secrecy exemption of the FOIA, to employ copyright protection, and, if these alternatives fail, to seek special statutory protection.

The status of scientific information with respect to trade secrecy has been subject to much discussion and conflicting interpretation. The most widely accepted definition of a trade secret used in tort law is "any formula, pattern, device, or compilation of information which is used in one's business, and which gives him an opportunity to obtain an advantage over competitors, who do not know or use it. It may be a formula for a chemical compound, a process of manufacturing, treating, or preserving materials, a pattern for a machine . . . ."[21] No fewer than 68 provisions in the federal statutes protect trade secrets from routine disclosure in litigation or under the FOIA.[22] However, these provisions are difficult to apply to research results with no immediate and obvious commercial value.

In 1967, the U.S. Attorney General interpreted the trade secrecy exemption of the FOIA to include "technical or scientific data or other information submitted in or with an application for a research grant or in or with a report while research is in progress."[23] However, the courts have not necessarily followed this interpretation. A much cited case involved a request by the Washington Research Project for information about eleven research projects funded by the National Institute of Mental Health.[24] The agency tried to protect the material, arguing that research constituted the scientists' "stock in trade" and was therefore equivalent to commercial information. Those who demanded access to the data, under the FOIA, argued that factual information in federal grant applications must be available and that the government's right of audit defined such material as an agency record. The U.S. Court of Appeals accepted the plaintiff's reasoning, ruling that the trade secrecy exemption of the FOIA, intended for commercial property, could not be extended to just any competitive activity:

> In considering exemption 4 for trade secrets or commercial information, the court found it irrelevant to inquire whether non-commercial scientists are either "a mean-spirited lot who pursue self-interest as ruthlessly as the Barbary pirates did in their own chosen field," or are governed by the loftier consideration that "secrecy is antithetical to the philosophical values of science."[25]

Reversing an earlier district court decision in the case, the appeals court ruled that without a specific showing of commercial value, research protocols, hypotheses, and designs submitted with federal grant applications were not entitled to protection from disclosure as trade secrets. Indeed, the judge declared, "It defies common sense to pretend that the scientist is engaged in trade or commerce."[26]

A bill to limit the use of the FOIA and clarify issues relevant to scientific research is under consideration in Congress. Proposed revisions include an extension of the exemption for trade secrecy to include preliminary research as well as trade secrets and financial or business information "the disclosure of which could impair the legitimate private competitive, research, financial, or business interests of any person . . . ."[27] Technical data—interpreted to include academic research—that falls under the scope of export control regulations would also be exempt from release under the revised act.

To a more limited extent, scientists have attempted to protect their research under the provisions of the copyright law. Designed to "protect original works of authorship fixed in any tangible medium of expression," copyright law applies in principle to data sets.[28] However, the "fair use" provisions of the copyright law allow the distribution of data for noncommercial scholarly purposes. Thus, for scientists concerned about priority in analyzing their data, copyrights do not adequately protect their rights. Moreover, the law, intended to ensure the "progress of science and the useful arts," has codified the distinction between an idea and its expression. Ideas or insights are part of the public domain; an author or scientist cannot protect the idea but only the form in which it appears.[29]

Ambiguities in copyright or trade secrecy law weaken their usefulness in protecting research. Scientists, therefore, have sought special statutory protection for both the information in research proposals and the data from long-term research projects. In 1977, the National Commission for the Protection of Human Subjects of Biomedical and Behavioral Research reviewed the use of the FOIA to request information in research protocols and designs. It deemed the federal policy of releasing data only after research funding was awarded to be appropriate and, indeed, necessary to protect peer review procedures. Disclosure earlier in the review process would be appropriate only with the consent of the investigator. The commission said the policy should apply to renewal applications as well. And the commission recommended legislation to ensure continuation of existing practice.[30]

In 1976, NIH requested a special amendment to the Public Health and Safety Act that would provide statutory protection for information arising from clinical trials. The NIH director also brought the matter before the Ethics Advisory Board of HEW, seeking to exempt clinical trials, epidemiological studies, and toxicological studies of drugs and chemicals—all long-term research in which premature and uncontrolled disclosure could be disruptive. He sought to establish the principle that data which are preliminary, incomplete, or not yet validated should be protected and that until the scientific community could establish the statistical significance of data from repeated trials, data should not be released. He argued that premature release of such data could result in the destruction of randomized clinical trials or in the identification of misleading trends that could unduly alarm the public.

The NIH director also feared that early disclosure of data would have a chilling effect on scientific participation in the research. Scientists engaged in such research must necessarily accept long delays before publication of findings, and FOIA requests for early release of data might discourage them from doing this research. In the long run, he argued, exemption from disclosure of data from clinical trials would provide better and more reliable information to the public and, therefore, is not in conflict with the intention of the FOIA.

The Ethics Advisory Board recommended legislation to provide a limited exemption on the following conditions: that the trial is ongoing and there is a legitimate requirement to maintain the confidentiality of interim data, that the confidential aspects of the study design are known in advance to the research participants as part of the procedure of informed consent, and that a qualified person or committee monitor emerging trends in order to judge whether or not the trial should be continued.[31]

The degree of required public access to research will be clarified if research methodologies and results are exempted from FOIA requests as are trade secrets and commercial interests. However, many questions would remain: At a time when the provisions for public access under the FOIA are threatened by bureaucratic obstruction if not political extinction, should scientists be seeking to limit the act further? Does the investment of time and ideas in fact constitute privilege? And if so, for how long? At what point in the research process is a scientist or a federal official obliged to release data?

The most difficult question is, Who is to decide? Scientists assume that the timing of disclosure and the content of what is to be released should remain in their control—that is, that the public interest would be better served by scientific sovereignty. In many cases this may be true, but this assumption also leads to a fundamental contradiction: the use of secrecy to maintain sovereignty within a community whose work is based on open communication of research findings.

Phillips Memorial
Library
Providence College

4. Rights of Access Versus Obligations of Confidentiality

In 1971 political scientist Samuel Popkin of Harvard University was called before a federal grand jury investigating the publication of the "Pentagon papers."[1] Popkin had been doing research on political forces and social movements in Vietnam and on American policy in that country. The grand jury ordered him to disclose the identity of confidential sources of information as well as information he had collected during research on Vietnam. Popkin refused to answer seven of 126 questions and denied involvement in the publication of the Pentagon papers. He asserted his right to protect information obtained in confidence, and he claimed that the demands of the grand jury violated his rights to freedom of speech and freedom of the press under the First Amendment.

Popkin's colleagues rose to his defense, denouncing any effort to compel scholars to reveal their sources of information. However, on 21 November 1972, after a series of legal maneuvers, Popkin was imprisoned for contempt. Seven days later the government disbanded the grand jury investigation and Popkin was released, but he petitioned the Supreme Court to review the case. Popkin did not try to establish a scientist's absolute right to refuse to testify before a grand jury; rather, he asked for a test that would balance the First Amendment rights of the scholar with the needs of the grand jury. Such a test would consider the importance of the information to the subject under investigation, the relevance of the information to a violation of the law, and the ability to obtain the information without infringing on First Amendment rights. The petition was denied.

The Popkin case tested the limits to the scholar's right to testimonial privilege—that is, the right of a researcher to claim immunity from the requirement to reveal names or other identifying information in legal proceedings. Other cases, less dramatic and less politically charged, have tested the rights of investigators to protect the privacy of their research sources against administrative requests.

In 1976, the National Heart and Lung Institute (NHLI) of the National Institutes of Health supported a longitudinal study of the health history of individuals with certain medical profiles. The researcher maintained detailed personal records but had to comply with requirements of the Privacy Act to protect the identity of subjects. As slated in his contract, he submitted only the final report of his findings to NHLI. During the course of the study an independent researcher in heart diseases requested access to the records for his own research. The first investigator, concerned about maintaining the confidentiality of his subjects, objected to opening his files. The agency decided, on the basis of the research contract, that decisions about the release of data were within the contractor's discretion. In this case, the researcher was allowed to decide whether or not data gathered to fulfill a federal contract could be released for other purposes and, more importantly, how to comply with the rules and regulations governing disclosure of confidential personal information.[2]

In other cases, however, federal agencies have tried to maintain more direct control. For example, in 1974, the Department of Health, Education, and Welfare (HEW, now Health and Human Services) and the National Science Foundation (NSF) awarded parallel research grants for evaluation studies of research methodologies to a team of sociologists headed by Donald McTavish at the University of Minnesota. The research, administered through a private organization, Minnesota Systems Research Incorporated (MSRI), was an effort to develop a method for predicting the quality of a project from various elements in the submitted proposals. The study required interviewing both principal investigators and those who rated the projects.

To obtain candid responses, the interviewers claimed to have guaranteed confidentiality to the agency officials who helped to identify projects and to have promised to protect the identity of the people interviewed. Several months before the project was complete, HEW asked for the computer tapes, which contained the names of the projects studied and the respondents. What happened in response to this request remains in dispute. According to McTavish, HEW also asked for data that would identify the independent raters, but he had scrambled the identity codes so that these could not be retrieved. However, according to the HEW general counsel, the agency had respected McTavish's pledge of confidentiality, though

it questioned whether MSRI had in fact promised confidentiality at all.

The investigators claimed to have established a prior
understanding with HEW about protecting the identities
of specific projects, but HEW insisted that a researcher
could not promise confidentiality without obtaining
prior written permission from the agency and that evaluation projects were not covered by privacy law. "The
attempt to bind the government to honor unauthorized
assurances of confidentiality . . . sets a poor precedent
for the free and unrestricted flow of research results and
the replicability of scientific studies."[3]

The investigators resisted the agency's demands, arguing that the project was a grant and accepted in that
spirit despite the practical interest of HEW in its results.
But in the agency view, the public interest requires that
the federal government have sufficient access to research
data to audit the expenditure of federal funds, to evaluate
the research it supports, and to ensure the protection of
research subjects.

After prolonged negotiation, MSRI released the tapes
to HEW. To McTavish the outcome suggested that "increasingly, investigators may find themselves without
effective means for protecting research subjects from
abuses by federal funding agencies who at their convenience profess to champion research ethics."[4]

Disputes over data are especially problematic when
they threaten the obligations of researchers to protect
the confidentiality of their sources of information. In the
process of doing research, scientists in some fields necessarily invade the privacy of subjects or receive information which, if disclosed, would put a subject in jeopardy,
legally or in some other way. In the cases just described,

the investigators promised confidentiality and asserted their right to control access to their records. Testimonial privilege for researchers is clearly limited. The extent of administrative control over confidential data, however, appears to rest on agency discretion.

Protecting the Sources of Data

Conflicts over confidentiality are most common in medical or social science research projects that require information about individual health or personal behavior.[5] Social scientists often rely on personal interviews, and by participating in a study, those who provide information may put themselves at risk. Answering questions about personal habits may later be a source of embarrassment. Revealing information about health problems or working conditions may cost a research subject his job, his credit rating, or his welfare status. In some cases, the subject may risk legal complications. Research subjects often take such risks with no reward except the understanding that participation may serve the public interest.

To obtain data, and sometimes simply to get an interview, the researcher must often promise confidentiality. Trust is necessary in such research. As sociologist Seymour Martin Lipset asserted with reference to the Popkin case:

It is a canon in this type of scholarly research that the investigator formally or implicitly guarantee anonymity to his respondents. That is, he assures them that if they will cooperate with him, no statement made to him will ever be transmitted to a third person identified as coming from a particular person. Much social science research . . . would be impossible unless such assurances are given.[6]

And as political scientist James Q. Wilson has stated:

A scholar who knowingly violates the confidence imparted to him is guilty of a grave ethical infraction; a society that requires a scholar to violate such a confidence in the absence of any showing that the information sought is directly and materially relevant to a criminal act is guilty of placing an unwarranted burden on free inquiry and academic responsibilities.[7]

The Popkin case is not unique; social scientists are often pressured to disclose information about their sources of data, especially when their research is in conflict with political or policy goals. For example, a judge asked the Kinsey Institute for Sex Research to reveal information about the individuals who participated in a controversial study of sexual practices. Federal agencies tried to subpoena records from various studies of campus unrest in the 1960s, records that detailed the actions of specific individuals. A county prosecutor, investigating state welfare payments in New Jersey, subpoenaed case records from a research project evaluating the state's negative income-tax experiment; the records contained information on the participants' earnings, their attitudes toward work, and the number of hours they worked.[8]

One study found that, between 1966 and 1976, at least 50 scholars were served subpoenas in 18 different cases, ordering them to reveal the identities of sources and subjects of research; another 30 scientists were threatened with subpoenas.[9] In a national survey of 314 researchers, 7.6 percent reported problems of maintaining confidentiality. The problems included wiretapping and direct pressure from government officials who were seeking raw data from politically sensitive projects on such topics as urban gangs, social welfare experiments, teenage unemployment, crime victimization, and compulsory school busing.[10]

Studies of deviant or politically sensitive groups are especially vulnerable. Under federal law, research on crime, drug addiction, and mental illness must include guarantees to protect the privacy of research subjects who might be subject to social or legal pressures should their identity be revealed. Scientists engaged in research on mental health can obtain certificates of confidentiality from the Department of Health and Human Services, which provide immunity from subpoenas. The Department of Justice can provide grants of confidentiality to protect data gathered in research projects involving drugs.[11] However, release of data from sociological and epidemiological studies that use medical records and personal data can be equally damaging to the individuals involved, and their anonymity is not protected against subpoena.

The laws governing confidentiality in research are inconsistent and often fail to honor a scientist's obligation to protect the anonymity of his research sources when this requirement is in conflict with the demands of the state. The National Research Act of 1974 requires that institutional review boards determine that projects contain adequate provisions to protect the privacy of research subjects and to maintain the confidentiality of data. However, neither this act nor the regulations protecting the privacy of medical information used in health research grants researchers and their data immunity from subpoena. Whenever researchers seek privilege from testifying in order to avoid compromising their research subjects or their sources of data, they may run into conflict with law enforcement agencies, policy decisions, or in some cases the need of a government agency to evaluate the work of a scientist it supports.

In lieu of statutory protections against subpoena, most laws concerning the confidentiality of research protect only the data collected and possessed by the government itself. Ironically, these laws often serve to restrict research. For example, the Privacy Act of 1974 restricts access to government administrative records that would identify individuals when access would violate their right to privacy.[12] Before information can be released, individuals must give written consent. The many exemptions to the Privacy Act include cases where access is necessary to enforce civil or criminal law, but the act does not allow access simply for purposes of research.

Scientists take issue with restrictions on their access to data, arguing that aggregate data, without identification of individuals, are inadequate for many kinds of research. Leon Gordis and Ellen Gold, epidemiologists at Johns Hopkins University, point out that research in their field must correlate the medical histories of individuals with records of their exposure to disease in order to compare sick and well people and to evaluate different approaches to prevention, detection, and treatment of disease.[13] Access to records that contain identities is thus essential, despite the potential risks to the individuals should their identity be more broadly disclosed.

Negotiations

Concerns about confidentiality have given rise to

many efforts to protect researchers from compulsory disclosure of information gathered in the course of research. These range from practices of defensive recordkeeping to legislative proposals.

To reduce the identifying characteristics of data, researchers have begun using various coding techniques, complex filing systems, and overseas storage of data. In some cases, data have even been destroyed in order to avoid the potential threat of subpoena. Recently, statistical methods with a randomized response approach have been developed to help preserve privacy. These methods allow an identified respondent to provide information in a way that permits statistical analysis of group data without revealing the individual state.[14]

Special committees of professional societies are considering guidelines to help members resolve problems of confidentiality. For example, the Society for Epidemiological Research is working with university departments of epidemiology to design specific methods to protect the confidentiality of research subjects. Several associations are experimenting with codes of ethics that would include provisions about disclosure when confidentiality is at stake. Such a code, sanctioned by a professional association, might at least provide support for a researcher pressured to release confidential information.

Scientists have also proposed research agreements that would confer a status of executive privilege on the research in order to protect confidentiality, but such proposals are not legally binding. According to Paul Nejelski, a lawyer experienced in confidentiality disputes, legislation is the only effective route for protection. He suggests that the Supreme Court decision that established the limits of the privileges of journalists to protect their sources, may be applicable to researchers as well.[15] In 1972 in the Branzburg case,[16] the Supreme Court upheld the general thrust of legal decisions that require journalists to testify in grand jury proceedings, but the court explicitly stated that Congress could create statutory privilege for those who serve to inform the public. The court placed a variety of professions in this category: "The information function assumed by representatives of the organized press in the present case is also performed by lecturers, political pollsters, novelists, academic researchers, and dramatists." And the court turned to Congress for guidance through legislation: "Congress has the freedom to determine whether a statutory newsman's privilege is necessary and desirable and to fashion standards and rules as narrow and broad as deemed necessary to address the evil discerned."[17]

Several statutes have been proposed to protect confidentiality in research situations. In 1975, a National Academy of Sciences committee proposed legislation that would protect from subpoena all information gathered during the course of research, including material that could identify subjects, and all observations, unfinished manuscripts, and notes preliminary to a final report. This proposal was not pursued, but in 1980, Congress considered several bills to protect confidentiality.

One bill, the Privacy of Research Records Act, was intended to exempt researchers from subpoena if testimony would violate the privacy of their subjects. Subjects of drug and alcohol research are already protected; this act would have extended protection to subjects of all federally funded research.[18] It also contained provisions to bar scientists from contacting subjects of earlier research without the approval of a review board and to require researchers to sign confidentiality pledges before using files compiled by other researchers. Investigators violating confidentiality would be subject to criminal penalties. The Privacy of Research Records Act never got as far as a hearing.

A companion bill on the confidentiality of medical records proposed that medical care facilities could disclose medical records of patients without their consent for use in research if the research was deemed important by an institutional review board. This bill was defeated in the House of Representatives.[19]

The control of and access to research data on identifiable subjects pose several dilemmas. The public benefit of scientific research may conflict with the risks of disclosure to the research subjects or others who contribute to the research. The public need for disclosure, especially in court, may conflict with the need to maintain the anonymity of sources and the privacy of subjects. To compound the problem, the principle of confidentiality can be easily perverted. It has been used deliberately to maintain secrecy in order to avoid competition, to prevent legitimate evaluation, and to protect institutional reputations.[20]

As some private and professional groups seek to develop ad hoc remedies to assist members who face pressures to release data, many scientists have come to believe that the problem requires protective legislation. In seeking statutory guarantees to the problem of protecting their sources of data, however, researchers must necessarily weigh conflicting interests, for the need to maintain confidentiality to protect research subjects may directly conflict with the public good.

5. Whistleblowing Versus Proprietary Rights

In 1964, Thomas Mancuso, of the University of Pittsburgh, began a long-term study on the effects of low-dose radiation on the health and mortality rates of the employees of Atomic Energy Commission (AEC) contractors. His work was supported by a research contract from the commission, and later its successors, the Energy Research and Development Agency and the Department of Energy (DOE). Mancuso followed the medical history of 35,000 workers at the Hanford Nuclear Facility in Washington State and 112,000 at the Oak Ridge National Laboratories in Tennessee. His study[1] was limited to workers with exposures of no more than two to three rads in a five year period, a level defined as safe in AEC guidelines. His preliminary findings showed no negative health effects, and his contract was renewed regularly for ten years.

In 1974, an epidemiologist in Washington, working independently, reported an excessive incidence of occupationally related cancer among Hanford workers.[2]

DOE pushed Mancuso to publish his preliminary findings in order to refute this report, but he refused. Later, Mancuso brought in Alice M. Stewart, of Birmingham University (UK), to do an independent analysis. She found evidence supporting a cancer effect due to radiation. DOE terminated Mancuso's contract and transferred the study first to the Oak Ridge National Laboratories and later to Battelle Northwest Laboratories. DOE justified the decision by asserting that Mancuso's work had received a negative technical evaluation, that he was reluctant to publish his findings or analyze his data until the work was complete, and that, in any case, he was about to retire. Mancuso denied his intention to retire and explained his reluctance to publish his early findings on the grounds that this would be premature and misleading in light of the long latency period of cancer. The agency had publicly denied the possibility of harmful occupational effects and Mancuso believed that DOE had terminated his contract in order to maintain direct control over future research.[3]

Mancuso later published research results indicating that there was a positive association between exposure to low levels of radiation and an increased incidence of cancer.[4] Mancuso also cooperated with an investigation conducted by the General Accounting Office by giving them his data on Hanford employees. DOE attempted to confiscate Mancuso's Hanford data and currently denies him access to data which he assembled on the Oak Ridge population.[5]

In 1980, Morris Baslow, a research biologist, was employed as a senior scientist in a private consulting firm that was working on environmental impact studies for Consolidated Edison. Con Ed, seeking to exempt one of its power plants from regulations requiring a back-fit cooling tower system, looked to the data developed by Baslow's firm on the effects of heated effluent on marine life to support its claim to an exemption. Baslow, however, contended that the firm's report, showing that the thermal effluent from the power plant caused only negligible damage to larvae and fish eggs in the river, had neglected crucial data from his own research. He had found that larvae and fish growth depended on optimal temperatures and that any increase in temperature might inhibit growth. The firm claimed Baslow's findings were unconfirmed and were, therefore, left out of the report.[6]

Baslow tried but failed to get permission from his firm to present his data at an Environmental Protection Agency (EPA) public hearing. In October 1979, he finally sent a letter questioning the validity of the firm's analysis directly to the EPA administrative law judge in charge of the hearing. That was his last day at work. Baslow took with him the papers documenting his temperature data and mailed copies to EPA and the Federal Energy Regulatory Commission (FERC). Unemployed, he sought compensation through the Department of Labor under the employee protection section of the Federal Water Pollution Control Act Amendments. The Labor Department found that his firm had violated the provisions of the act by dismissing Baslow for releasing company records. However, the company claimed proprietary interest and work-product immunity in order to restrain further dissemination of the research and to regain possession of the documents which, they claimed, Baslow had stolen from his office.

The firm initiated a suit demanding return of the documents and asking $5.2 million in damages. Baslow, as the researcher, claimed that the information in the documents belonged to him. EPA filed a legal brief supporting Baslow. Depending on the integrity of scientific information presented in regulatory proceedings, the agency was anxious to protect those who brought their research data to hearings. FERC also supported Baslow by rejecting the company's claim of proprietary interest and work-product immunity, thereby settling the ownership dispute. Baslow, however, agreed in settlement out of court to return his documents to the company in order to protect himself against costly libel proceedings.[7] The Baslow case raised a number of points only partially resolved by the agency decisions. For example, Can a firm withhold preliminary and even unconfirmed data that may be relevant to a matter under agency investigation? And what alternatives are available to someone like Baslow who is convinced that his firm's data are seriously incomplete?

Many other cases have centered on the right of scientists to use their knowledge or research in the public interest.[8] In 1981, Peter Infante, an epidemiologist at the Occupational Safety and Health Administration (OSHA), went outside agency channels by publicly asserting that formaldehyde was a carcinogen. A substantial scientific consensus on the carcinogenicity of formaldehyde supported his claim. However, when a group of industrial scientists from the Formaldehyde Institute questioned the validity of his data and complained directly to the OSHA administrator, Infante received notification of dismissal for insubordination. Later, under a great deal of pressure from scientists, OSHA backed away from the issue and Infante retained his job.[9]

Whistleblowing Disputes

Whistleblowing disputes arise in several situations. In

some cases, a scientist goes public, revealing data or calling public attention to a problem by going to the press or to public officials outside the normal channels of technical communication.[10] These channels are felt to be too cumbersome in light of the urgency of the situation and the risks that may be involved. The release of data about Love Canal or toxic shock syndrome, for example, could not wait for peer review.

In other instances, scientists call public attention to data that have been suppressed because of the interests of an agency or firm, as in the Mancuso case. And sometimes, as in the Baslow case, whistleblowing disputes occur when scientists disagree with the official reporting of their data and want to publicize a dissenting view.

In each type of dispute, concerned scientists try to publicize the knowledge available to them because they believe it to be in the public interest. They are prevented from doing so by their employers or contractors—in some cases, private firms, in others, government agencies. The majority of scientists today work under specific contracts or directly for agencies, industries, or consulting firms, where the employers or contractors assume that they have a right to control decisions about dissemination of data. However, scientists who try to disclose controversial data appeal to the value of openness in science, their right to freedom of expression, and their moral responsibility to disclose information that would provide an early warning of potential harm.

Some whistleblowing episodes occur within science, exposing cases of fraud, falsification of data, or sloppy research practices. A rash of such episodes has come to public view.[11] A biologist at Harvard University substituted monkey cells for human cells in a study of Hodgkins disease. A researcher at Sloan-Kettering Cancer Institute painted spots on mice to demonstrate the success of skin grafts. A scientist at Boston University tampered with the charts of his research subjects in a study of a drug to retard the growth of cancer cells. A Yale University scientist fabricated data and plagiarized the work of a younger colleague. A Harvard Medical School researcher altered his data on the effect of drugs on heart disease.

In 1977, two doctoral students reported irregularities in the research practices of a professor. They alleged that he had misled research subjects who had donated blood for a study of sickle cell anemia and had failed to obtain their informed consent. An investigating committee found that the scientist had avoided the prior review required when research involves human subjects. However, the committee concluded that the research did not endanger the subjects. The students have since claimed that they suffered reprisals—harassment, lawsuits, and denial of research funds.[12]

Such incidents are occurring in intensely competitive and rapidly developing areas of research where the possibilities of replication and rigorous verification are limited. Perhaps because of the tradition of individual sovereignty, scientists have been reluctant to acknowledge fraud publicly. The scientist who faked his data on Hodgkins disease had been caught before in a similar incident, yet he was encouraged to continue his research. Several scientists fired for falsifying data found positions at other laboratories. In some cases, research funding and institutional support for a scientist accused of falsifying data has continued without interruption. It is assumed that deviance can be controlled through the self-correcting process of peer review.

In April 1981, the House Committee on Science and

Technology held hearings on the apparently growing incidence of fraud. The purpose was to determine whether such incidents were simply "episodes that will drift into the history of science as footnotes or whether we are creating situations and incentives in the biomedical sciences, and all of 'Big Science' that make such cases as these the 'tip of the iceberg.'"[13] At the hearings, scientists dismissed episodes of fraud as "aberrations," "rare acts," and "cases of psychopathic behavior." They blamed the problem on the external pressures on science, the tensions in the work environment, the competition for grant funds, the insecurity about careers, and the reduced contact between overworked scientists and their graduate or postdoctoral students who do much of the actual research. Those who point out cases of fraud are regarded by their colleagues with profound ambivalence, sometimes as disloyal scientists who draw public attention to the internal problems of science, or sometimes as "Paul Revere[s] who sound the tocsin against an imminent danger."[14] Whistleblowing disputes are a manifestation of a broader dilemma: the problem of disclosing information in the public interest when disclosure conflicts with proprietary claims.

We know that nondisclosure of information can have devastating consequences. When an Italian scientist failed to disclose publicly his findings on the carcinogenicity of vinyl chloride, thousands of workers continued to be exposed to the chemical without adequate protection.[15] In 1972, Cesare Maltoni, working on research sponsored by several European chemical companies, found angiosarcoma and other cancers of the liver and kidneys in experimental animals that had been exposed to vinyl chloride at concentrations of 250 parts per million. The permitted exposure level for workers was 500 parts per million. Maltoni, who worked under a secrecy agreement with European manufacturers, was not to disclose his findings without permission. The European companies gave the U.S. Manufacturing Chemists Association information on the studies on the condition that it be kept confidential. Not until 1974, when deaths of workers at a B. F. Goodrich plant from angiosarcoma of the liver were reported, was the research made public. Then other vinyl chloride manufacturers reported problems, and OSHA lowered the permissible exposure level. Clearly, in this case release of data would have served the public well.

Another reported situation of nondisclosure borders on the absurd. In 1979, the New York State Department of Health and Hooker Chemical Corporation initiated separate health studies on workers who had been exposed to pesticides, solvents, and defoliants. To conduct their epidemiological study of the health of past employees, the Department of Health needed data on employees from Hooker's personnel files. It could then compare these data with cases in the state cancer registry. Hooker, in turn, needed access to the state's cancer registry. Each group had information that was essential to the other's study, but neither would cooperate, and each denied all requests for information. In effect, nondisclosure of data had precluded a thorough study of occupational health.[16]

Data from the health and safety testing of new products such as food additives, drugs, and chemicals are often the focus of proprietary disputes, especially when powerful economic interests are at stake. Disclosure of test information on safety may reduce commercial incentives for new product development by opening trade secrets to competitors. Licensing drugs requires years and years of testing at a cost of millions of dollars. During this time, trade secrecy is often the only proprietary protection. Disclosure, it is argued, would erode the ability of companies to reap the economic benefits of their work.

Following this logic, the chemical industry proposed legislation to amend the Federal Insecticide, Fungicide, and Rodenticide Act (FIFRA). The amendment, which was eventually defeated, called for a five-year secrecy period for "innovative methods of using new technology." This would have effectively restricted independent scientific review of the product-testing data that are submitted to the EPA and would have denied to consumers and regulators the opportunity to make informed decisions about potential risks. It would also have removed the public pressure to improve agency decisions. In such cases, the confidentiality required by trade secrecy protection conflicts directly with the principle of disclosure in the public interest.

Congress has insisted that health and safety data cannot be classed as proprietary information. Requirements for disclosure of data are coupled with provisions for a period of "exclusive use" to ensure that, by releasing health and safety information, a firm does not lose its proprietary rights. Congress, however, has not addressed closely related problems concerning the health and safety of new drugs.[17]

Discouraging Disclosure

Those who would disclose information outside normal channels in order to bring data on potentially harmful industrial or research practices to public view often face unexpected reprisals, repercussions, and social pressures. Professionals who work as public employees and who may be torn between conflicting obligations to their employers and to the public interest face special problems. But scientists outside the government may also be restrained by the need to protect future contractual arrangements with their government or industry research sponsors. Competition for research support encourages the resolution of problems of data control in favor of those who finance the research.

Public agencies, industries, and some scientists support measures to discourage whistleblowing on a number of grounds. Agencies responsible for regulation, for example, want to avoid premature disclosure of preliminary results that may later be unsubstantiated. They fear that whistleblowing about potential risks may create unnecessary public alarm, but they may be equally concerned that the exposure of embarrassing information would call attention to sloppy regulatory practices, to mismanagement, or to the existence of hazards that would be costly to control.

With the ushering in of the administration of President Ronald Reagan, agencies have become increasingly resistant to whistleblowing. At the Environmental Protection Agency, for example, there has been a major policy reversal. EPA had actively defended scientists who called attention to problems affecting the environment, but in September 1981, EPA's new research director, Andrew Jovanovich, circulated a plan to deter researchers from making public statements. Every oral presentation by an EPA scientist, consultant, or contractor was to be reviewed at four levels for inappropriate policy statements or conclusions.[18]

Industries hold that disclosure of data about potential risks may reveal proprietary information and that scientific evidence about environmental and public health hazards is often inconclusive. Value judgements may be involved in the interpretation of risks, and claims are difficult to document in definitive terms. Morris Baslow's firm questioned his interpretation of data about the effect of heated effluent on marine life, suggesting that the issue was merely a technical disagreement among scientists over the validity of data.

Scientists too may resent whistleblowers who disclose information about research problems. Preferring to deal with their problems within the limits of the scientific community, they resist publicity that could increase external surveillance and control over research in areas already monitored by commissions, committees, and specialty boards. They also worry about how to evaluate whistleblowers' claims. Is the scientist acting in good conscience or in pique? And suppose honest differences in scientific judgment are what is really at stake? These questions have engaged professional journals, as gatekeepers of scientific information, in disclosure disputes. Journal policies usually serve to discourage public-interest disclosure. If an investigator announces a finding to the press because of potential public interest in the issue, he may have to forego later publication of the finding in a peer-reviewed professional journal. Arnold Relman, editor of the *New England Journal of Medicine*, defends this so-called Ingelfinger rule, named for a former editor of the journal. Relman refuses to publish studies that have been previously released to the press, stating that this policy is the only way to preserve professional control and to prevent the dissemination of inaccurate, fraudulent, or incomplete research.[19] He feels that more harm than good can come from broadcasting opinions before they are professionally reviewed and published in the medical literature.

Sidney Wolfe, of the Public Citizens Health Research

Group, is among those who take a critical view of this policy.[20] He notes that whatever professional journals choose to do, people are continually exposed to, indeed bombarded with, scientific information and misinformation through advertising. Hardly subject to peer review, advertisements, especially for new drugs and so-called scientific cures, can be far more harmful than news stories. Thus, it is argued, efforts to restrict scientists' contacts with the press may do more harm than good.

Negotiations

Whistleblowers can be restrained by legal action as well as threats of reprisal, delayed publication, academic censure, or, ultimately, dismissal from a job. But they have no clear legal framework in which to seek protection or resolve whistleblowing disputes, and there are no adequate professional norms to guide scientists in deciding whether or when to blow the whistle.[21] Thus, there are many who argue that some adequate mechanisms to protect whistleblowers are needed in order to encourage public interest disclosure.

John Edsall, former chairman of the AAAS Committee of Scientific Freedom and Responsibility, asserts that: "It is obviously in the interest of public health and safety that [whistleblowers] should be heard and fairly judged; and if their views are upheld after a hearing by a suitable body, they deserve commendation, and perhaps promotion, not discharge."[22]

Encouraging the disclosure of data in the public interest requires that whistleblowers be protected. A number of efforts have been made with this in mind. In 1975, Senator Edward Kennedy introduced the Federal Employees Disclosure Act that would have protected federal employees who disclosed information which they considered to be in the public interest. This legislation failed to pass, but some public employees gained limited legal protection against reprisal for whistleblowing from the Civil Service Reform Act of 1978.[23] Protection is given only to federal employees working on biomedical research projects who disclose information about threats to public health or safety, illegal action, or mismanagement; other scientists working under NIH grants are not covered.

Several states have laws to protect employees from retaliation, but only one, Michigan, has a comprehensive Whistleblowers Protection Act covering employees in the private sector.

Some federal agencies have set up institutions to encourage whistleblowing, but they offer few protections. The Office for the Protection from Research Risks (OPRR), established in NIH in 1977, is authorized to investigate research violating federal regulations. With no subpoena power, OPRR depends on voluntary information; however, it has no authority to investigate charges of retaliation.

Professional societies are debating their role as intermediaries in disclosure disputes and their responsibility to develop guidelines and establish procedures to evaluate complaints. According to an AAAS survey, they face the issue with considerable ambivalence.[24] Should professional societies assist in conflicts that could expose ethical problems within the scientific community? Should they become involved in supporting the individual scientist as a moral agent, or should they restrict themselves to setting the standards to be followed by their members? The survey found that only 30 percent of the 146 societies that responded had established procedures to investigate disputes, and few had significant budgets devoted to such problems. The survey's author, Rosemary Chalk, suggests that more active professional support for public interest in required:

> Like the miner's canaries, scientists and engineers provide a vulnerable margin of sensitivity that may alert society as a whole to harmful uses of science and technology. . . . Providing them with legal protections and effective aid from their professional groups will held keep them in good voice.[25]

Whistleblowing cases are, in effect, disputes over the ownership or control of scientific information, for they challenge the freedom of scientists to disclose their knowledge and to interpret their data as they see fit. In the continued debates over disclosure of politically sensitive or proprietary information, the question of how to balance the public interest against proprietary claims remains unresolved. This question has become increasingly critical in light of the officially sanctioned withdrawal of information from public view. The Reagan administration has, for example, suspended labeling requirements for toxic chemicals and programs to inform workers of occupational risks. It has increased the levels of policy review to which government documents are subjected before they are released. It has impounded documents with data negative to prevailing policy views. It has essentially reversed a trend of the past twenty-five years toward increasing public information. In this context, efforts to reconcile public interest disclosure and proprietary claims are more important than ever.

6. National Security Versus Scientific Freedom

In the summer of 1980, Leonard Adleman, a mathematician working at both the Massachusetts Institute of Technology (MIT) and the University of Southern California (USC), applied to the National Science Foundation (NSF) for a grant in computer mathematics. The research was intended to provide a mathematical base for sophisticated computer techniques that would be impervious to code-breaking. Such research is useful for military purposes but also for the protection of banking records, medical dossiers, and other private information stored on computer tapes.

NSF routinely supports the kind of research Adleman proposed, but since 1977, it has sent all cryptography proposals to the National Security Agency (NSA) for technical review because of their potential significance in military intelligence. NSA, which uses code-breaking techniques to collect intelligence information, also does its own in-house research in cryptography, and it has become increasingly watchful of the expanding areas of basic mathematical research which are relevant to its intelligence-gathering concerns yet outside of its immediate purview.

In 1978, the agency had issued a secrecy order on an encrypting device developed at the University of Wisconsin, claiming it to be of potential military significance. The device was about to be patented when NSA intervened. The MIT project was, however, the first basic research to attract the agency's serious attention. NSA tried to take over a part of the project funding so that it could require review of the research for military sensitivity before publication. This suggested a new level of NSA control—over publication of scientific findings as well as over the patenting of actual devices.[1]

Although he eventually received an NSF grant, Adleman was appalled at the idea that his work might be classified, and therefore unpublishable and unavailable for public use. The issues raised by this incident are sensitive because of two apparent trends: first, to extend government control to research that is not sponsored by agencies concerned with national security and, second, to apply controls not only to hardware but also to basic ideas and strategic information—that is, to nonclassified information that if released could, in the judgment of the NSA, possibly harm the national interest. These trends imply prior constraints on publication of research and restrictions on scientific communication, both abhorrent and alien to the traditions of science.

Similar issues emerged in a well-publicized case in 1978 in which Howard Morland, a free-lance journalist, wrote an article on the construction and operation of the hydrogen bomb for *The Progressive*, a small journal with a circulation of about 40,000. The article relied entirely on nonclassified documents and sources in the public domain. Erwin Knoll, the editor of the journal, sent the piece to several government scientists, requesting verification of technical accuracy. He subsequently received a temporary restraining order from the Justice Department suppressing publication of the article on the grounds that it revealed secret, restricted data damaging to national security. The article could not be published, claimed government officials, because it could help foreign nationals develop the bomb.

The case became the focus of a debate over the misuse of secrecy procedures designed to protect information. Believing that government secrecy extended well beyond reasonable need, Knoll wanted to test the government's right to impose secrecy on all data pertaining to the design or use of nuclear weapons. The controversial article, claimed Knoll, contained nothing more than could be drawn from the *Encyclopedia Americana*. No one in the dispute, which went on for over seven months, contended that classified material had been used. Nevertheless, *The Progressive*'s effort "to demystify the issue of secrecy" raised a storm, pitting the right of the government to exercise prior restraint over publication against the First Amendment's protection of freedom of the press.[2] When a computer programmer with a hobby of collecting documents on nuclear weaponry published a long letter in a Madison, Wisconsin, newspaper, covering essentially the same material as the Morland article, the Justice Department withdrew its case. Though legally settled, the Department of Energy (DOE) asked for an investigation into the activities of participants in the *Progressive* case, including scientists in government laboratories who had cooperated with Morland or who had spoken up in support of the magazine.

The *Progressive* case dramatically drew public attention to the problems of attempting to repress privately developed information on nuclear weaponry. Knoll's effort to expose the fallacies of government secrecy received support from a wide variety of journals and organizations:

> In a time when military policy is closely linked with technological capabilities, debate about military policy that uses technical information is part of a vigorous system of freedom of expression under the First Amendment. The government's tendency to hide widely known technical processes under a mantle of secrecy in the national interest . . . can only result in stifling debate.[3]

On the other side were people—even those aware of the need to reduce secrecy and sympathetic to *The Progressive*'s goals—who nonetheless criticized the effort to publish the piece. They feared that government officials would use the example of a relative layman's ability to put together such an article from unclassified documents as evidence of the weakness of the security system; instead of demystifying secrecy, the article might encourage more stringent controls. This indeed seems to be the case.

Constraints on the publication and communication of work with potential military significance are obviously not new. Under the Invention Secrecy Act of 1952, patentable discoveries can be placed under secrecy orders if disclosure is deemed detrimental to national security.[4] This is normally enforced in the case of inventions developed by people working in defense agencies or under defense contracts, but it has been increasingly applied to other inventions as well. The Invention Secrecy

Act was invoked by NSA, for example, in order to classify the computer cipher device invented by the University of Wisconsin mathematician.

Formidable controls have always governed the secrecy of atomic research.[5] Since World War II, the federal government has held unambiguous authority to exercise control over all atomic research, whether conducted within or outside government laboratories. Indeed, all information pertaining to this area is "born" classified, although the controls have become more controversial with the development of nuclear energy for civilian use. The Atomic Energy Act of 1954 relaxed certain provisions to encourage commercial development, but federal controls still grant DOE proprietary interest in ideas in the field as well as freedom from outside scrutiny. Proprietary interest was the issue challenged in *The Progressive* incident.

The Atomic Energy Act was "deliberately designed to regulate the exchange of scientific ideas [and] to prescribe when and how a scientist may publish or otherwise communicate the results of his work,"[6] according to those who helped draft it. For the most part it has been administered with some restraint, but in 1950, it was successfully invoked to suppress the publication in *Scientific American* of an article on thermonuclear weapons by Hans Bethe. The injunction later imposed on *The Progressive* article was not an isolated act but a demonstration of the real authority of federal control over intellectual property in this field.

The government controls the export of technical information under the International Traffic in Arms Regulations (ITAR), developed as part of the Mutual Security Act of 1954 and largely superceded by the Arms

Export Control Act of 1976. Administered by the Department of State, these regulations cover the export of technical data, defined to include unclassified information useful in the design of "any technology which advances the state-of-the-art or establishes a new art in any area of significant military applicability."[7] Such information requires that papers be approved by a cognizant agency before publication.

The Export Administration Act of 1979 controls the export of goods and services that are not covered by ITAR.[8] This act is administered by the Department of Commerce, but the Department of Defense plays an active role in monitoring the controls. In principle, the act applies to information presented in conferences, lectures, and meetings and requires the secretary of the Department of Commerce to examine the export of all technical data, including the 1.5 million new scientific and technical articles that appear annually and are available for foreign review. Clearly, these layers of regulations are too cumbersome to be fully enforced. Yet the very inclusiveness of their provisions allows considerable flexibility of interpretation with respect to the definition of strategic information. Several incidents suggest the trend toward increasingly inclusive interpretation of these secrecy laws.

Controls on the Export of Information

In September 1980, the Department of Defense issued a brochure stating that scientific exchanges sponsored by the United States were enhancing Soviet military power and that the professional and open scientific literature was adverse to U.S. military security interests.[9] The bilateral science and technology exchange program had facilitated the meeting of some 250 different scientific working groups and had stimulated considerable research. The defense agency questioned the wisdom of this program and also the exchanges administered by the U.S. and Soviet academies of science, arguing that these were not really reciprocal because of Soviet restrictions on information: "The Soviets exploit scientific . . . exchanges in a highly orchestrated, centrally directed effort aimed at gathering the technical information required to enhance their military posture."[10]

In April 1982, an anonymous report, "Soviet Acquisition of Western Technology,"[11] attacked the Soviets' use of university laboratories, scientific exchanges, and conferences to advance their military capabilities and called for more restrictive measures on the U.S. scientific communities.

The concerns that resurfaced in this 1982 report had been evident in several earlier government actions. In the winter of 1980, the government imposed a series of restrictions on scientific exchange.[12] First, DOE issued an order requiring government clearance of any communication between its contractors and Soviet scientists. Then the Department of Commerce forced the American Vacuum Society to withdraw its invitation to Soviet bloc scientists to attend a small international conference on magnetic bubble memory devices—a technology useful in extending computer memory capability. The department asserted that "oral exchanges of information in the U.S. with foreign nationals constitute export of technical data."[13] The meeting thus fell under the purview of Export Administration Regulations, and the sponsors would have to obtain an export license before admitting the Soviet bloc scientists. The invitation was rescinded, and all other foreign participants at the conference had to sign an affidavit promising not to reveal information from the conference to scientists from the Soviet bloc.

Also that winter, the State Department refused to issue visas to eight Soviet scientists who planned to attend a conference on lasers and electro-optical systems sponsored by the Optical Society of America and the Institute of Electrical and Electronics Engineers. The restrictions were precipitated by the discovery that a Hungarian physicist had provided the Russians with information on magnetic bubble memories that he had acquired while in the United States. By the end of 1981, as part of the political and economic sanctions to be taken against the Soviet Union, President Ronald Reagan decided that exchange agreements between the United States and the Soviet Union would be allowed to lapse.

Foreign students also came under increasing scrutiny. Several proposals were put forward to require academic institutions which had foreign students in certain scientific fields to submit detailed information on what the students would be studying, who they would be working with, and where they planned to travel. State Department officials have urged academic departments to follow the movements of individual foreign students and visitors and to control their access to information. Universities, for example, have received directives from the State Department to limit activities of Soviet and Chinese visitors.[14] The State Department also demanded that a certain Russian organic chemist visiting MIT's Department of Nutrition be denied access to work on nutritional research. Stanford University received a request to restrict a Soviet robotics expert from access to computer research.

In the fall of 1981, the State Department moved to restrict the studies of a Chinese scholar in the computer science department at the University of Minnesota:

> It is suggested that Qi be restricted from any access to unpublished or classified government-funded work. It is also suggested that the program emphasize course work with minimal involvement in applied research. There should be no access to the design, construction, or maintenance data relevant to individual items of computer hardware. . . . This office should be advised prior to any visit to any industrial or research facilities.[15]

The President of the University, C. Peter McGrath, responded:

> We are insistent that our faculty and our students be allowed to operate in their teaching and research functions both in title and in spirit in ways consistent with our academic traditions and the applicable laws which we believe are totally on the side of openness . . . .[16]

Other universities have also balked at such restrictions and have convinced the National Academy of Science to negotiate with the State Department. Although the Academy succeeded in getting the restrictions on the visit of the Soviet robotics expert relaxed, the directives continue, creating a real dilemma for foreign nationals—including over 2500 Chinese students—who comprise nearly a third of all science and engineering graduate students in American universities.

Legislative trends suggest that restrictions on scientific exchange may be formalized. The Department of Energy Authorization Act of 1982, for example, extends controls on unclassified information by prohibiting the unauthorized dissemination of unclassified information pertaining to the design of facilities or to security measures that could reasonably be expected to have a significant effect on public health and safety or the common defense.[17] The Export Administration Regulations have been further extended to cover ideas as well as hardware; that is, "information of any kind that can be used, or adapted for use, in the design, production, manufacture, utilization or reconstruction of articles or materials."[18]

The most comprehensive legislative proposal to date (H.R. 109, introduced in 1981) is an extension of the provisions of the Arms Export Control Act, which requires a license from the State Department to export "critical technology." The proposed changes would redefine the class of transactions subject to licensing requirements to include unclassified data and ideas that might pertain to military technology. Scientists who want to publish research or speak overseas on any subject relating to a technology listed in the United States munitions list would have to obtain a license from the Secretary of Defense in consultation with the Secretary of State and the Secretary of Energy. Restricted subjects could include all research related to computers, lasers, and cryptography, but the listings and their scope are far from clear.

Ambiguities increased with the creation in 1980 of the military critical technologies list, a classified document intended to supplement the munitions list and reported to include some 700 technologies. Scientists working in potentially sensitive areas would bear the burden of proof to show that dissemination of their work would not impair national security and that withholding the information would itself be contrary to the national interest.[19]

Revisions are also proposed for the Export Administration Act, extending restrictions of export data to cover unpublished written matter such as notes or drafts. A Justice Department review notes that the proposed licensing requirements apply to activities that are protected under the Constitution; the restrictions may therefore violate constitutional rights.[20]

While the proposed legislative revisions languishe⸱ in congressional committee, they were superceded by an executive order that has greatly increased government powers to classify research, even in areas that are not clearly related to national security. Every President since Harry Truman has issued executive orders that have limited classification by sharpening the standards necessary to classify and reducing the authority to classify. This thirty-year trend to extend public access and prevent unnecessary classification has been abruptly reversed.

Executive Order 12356 allows the government to classify any federally funded research even when the funding agency has no classification authority, thereby covering NSF-funded cryptography research. In fact, all government grantees are personally responsible for complying with classification constraints if they have any reason to believe that their work has security implications. The executive order also allows classification of nongovernment research and writing even when this is based on nonclassified information, thereby covering cases such as *The Progressive* article. It also drops two critical requirements established by the Carter administration: that classification requires evidence of "identifiable" damage to national security and that decisions imposing secrecy must be balanced against the public's right to know. And to cover any contingencies, the order mandates that, "if

there is reasonable doubt about the need to classify
information . . . the information shall be considered
classified."[21]

The all-encompassing character of the executive order
provoked an angry response from the Congress. The
House Government Operations Committee deplored the
secrecy in which the order was created with only minimal consultation with Congress or the public, and criticized the trend toward over-classification that would unnecessarily restrict public availability of information and
ultimately weaken the protection of truly sensitive material.[22]

Negotiations

The new restrictions, both those proposed and those
in place, are consistent. They reflect a coherent effort to
extend military controls to scientific communication not
explicitly related to military purposes. Government officials explain such constraints in vivid metaphors that
reveal their underlying perceptions and concerns: they
see a "hemorrhaging" of the nation's technologies, a
"leakage" of scientific ideas, a "siphoning away" of critical techniques. Scientific journals, meetings, and exchanges are seen as "mines of information," to be ex-
ploited by the Soviet Union to its own advantage.

In a speech delivered in 1982, former Deputy Director
of the Central Intelligence Agency Admiral Bobby Inman acknowledged the tension between "the scientist's
desire for unconstrained research and publication . . . and the federal government's need to protect
certain information from potential foreign adversaries
who might use that information against this nation."[23]
Inman saw a direct conflict between science, with its

tradition of open publication, and national defense needs.

Many scientists argue that this perception is naive and uninformed. While admitting that there may be security risks, they claim that technological leadership depends on the open communication that helps transform ideas into technology. Secrecy would weaken this system, stifling the scientific endeavor, reducing innovation, and, in the long run, undermining the national interest. Other scientists, concerned that the government has no real case beyond its desire to control information, respond with outrage to the very idea of secrecy. They claim that secrecy violates the principles of science as an activity based on the free exchange of ideas and that research, by definition, must be open and shared. They believe that scientists the world over share a common culture: that as an international resource in the public domain, science must stand above political turmoil and cannot be tied to political events.[24] Clearly, negotiations must reconcile, not polarize, positions.

In his 1982 presentation, Inman urged scientists to establish a system of voluntary restraint that would allow prepublication review of research that has potential military significance. Confrontation instead of cooperation, he warned, would bring a "tidal wave of public outrage," which could lead to stringent legislative solutions.

Inman based his idea of voluntary censorship on the system he tried to establish to resolve the cryptography dispute.[25] Mathematicians formed the Public Cryptography Study Group to decide how to meet the need for free and unrestrained research while protecting data in the national interest. The National Security Agency (NSA) proposed a voluntary system in which individual researchers would submit their papers to the agency in advance of publication for review of possible security implications. NSA conceded that if there are objections to proposed changes or potential security problems that would restrict publication, the papers would be sent for review to a special advisory committee of five members, two appointed by the NSA and three by the President's science advisor from a list provided by the National Academy of Sciences. This voluntary system has been criticized by several prominent mathematicians working in the cryptology field. The American Mathematical Society has adopted a neutral position, leaving it to the individual researchers to decide whether or not to comply with the NSA plan.[26]

Other proposals to reconcile the conflict between open research and security restrictions include a change in the peer review process so that the question of potential harm to national security would be considered before research is begun. Along these lines, the counsel for the Department of Defense has proposed that that agency's research awards contain stipulations restricting publication and access by foreign visitors. This idea of prior restraint contradicts scientific values, and it is the policy of most universities to turn down contracts that do not give scientists final authority over publication. Indeed, unrestricted publication is one of the factors that attracts scientists to academic research. It is widely believed that policies of prior review would result in decisions favoring censorship over academic freedom.

University administrations face several dilemmas in negotiating their case. Restrictions on research applicable to military systems are forcing the sharpening of distinctions between basic and applied research. When the presidents from five major universities voiced their concern to the State Department about the extension of export rules, officials assured them that the rules would apply only to research applied to technology and not to basic theoretical work. A panel of civilian scientific advisors to the Defense Science Board recommended to Congress that clear guidelines distinguish basic research and research applicable to military systems. Executive Order 12356, which does distinguish basic from applied research, claims to cover only the latter.

Although such distinctions are a means for protecting basic science, it is increasingly difficult to separate militarily critical information from the the general body of scientific knowledge. Both the basic and the applied sciences gain from flexible and easy exchange with each other. However, if such exchanges lead to security restrictions, they may be avoided. This would be costly to both types of research. Paradoxically, the distinctions encouraged by restrictions are also likely to weaken the desirable goal of using science as a spur to technological innovation.

Scientists face yet another dilemma because of their economic vulnerability. At a time of relatively scarce resources, scientific dependence on military research support is growing. Little more than a decade ago academia's role in military research was a contentious and polarizing issue on university campuses, but today the Pentagon and some universities are seeking ways to build partnerships in research and development related to national security. Many are convinced that the alliance is needed both to support graduate education and to meet the scientific and engineering manpower needs of government, industry, and the national defense.[27]

The expansion of university research in the 1950s was largely the result of support from the military. The ties between universities and the defense establishment were mutually rewarding. In the context of the times, most university scientists supported collaboration with military objectives, a collaboration they deemed crucial to the development of the nation's scientific abilities. However, even during this period, university-military relationships were a source of nagging concern. Doubts turned to disenchantment during the Vietnam War.[28] The Mansfield Amendment to the 1969 Department of Defense authorization bill specified that money funneled to universities by the Department of Defense be limited to projects with a "direct and apparent relationship to specific military function or operation." This contributed to the decline in military-funded university research. Between 1965 and 1975, defense funds for research and development in universities were reduced from nearly $300 million to $200 million. At the time, alternative sources of federal research support were available, and, anxious to quell the controversies over military research, universities showed little concern about reduction of these funds.

The picture has changed. The military is eager to reestablish useful relationships, and the universities need research support. For the Pentagon, academic liaisons are desirable as a direct source of high technology knowhow and trained technical personnel. Military power depends on advanced technology in areas such as computer analysis and fiber optics, which also have applications beyond the military and cannot easily be limited to government laboratories. Thus defense funding of university research, especially in microelectronics, aeronautics, and computer science, has increased to two-thirds of its pre-1969 level (in constant dollars). Further increases in military support of university research seem likely. A Defense Science Board Task Force on university

responsiveness to national security requirements has recommended more funding targeted towards critical military needs, promotion of closer ties and long-term relationships between faculty and defense-related projects,
and increased support of graduate students in defense-
related programs.[29]

Many universities have welcomed renewed support
from the Defense Department. In 1981, the Association
of American Universities sent a delegation to the House
Armed Services Subcommittee on Research and Development to seek greater research funding from the Pentagon as a way to maintain the universities' research
capacity at a time of growing financial pressure.[30] Because of the instability of alternative sources of federal
research funds, outmoded equipment, a shortage of faculty in high-technology areas, and rising operating costs,
there appears to be little speculation or concern among
academic scientists about the long-term implications of
many of these commitments. Despite complaints about
government-imposed restrictions on open communication through ITAR and export controls, the secrecy
implications of increased dependence on the military as
the contractor of academic research are generally ig-
nored.[31]

These implications were suggested by the DOD's first
major effort to implement legislative controls preventing
the unauthorized disclosure of technical data that could
be of military use. In August 1982, the Society of Photo-
Optical Instrumentation Engineers held its annual international symposium in San Diego, California, with more
than 2700 participants from 25 countries. Two weeks
before the conference, the Pentagon officials who reviewed the work supported by military contracts concluded that many of the papers required a license under

the ITAR regulations. The Pentagon and the Department of Commerce warned the speakers to adhere to regulations on technology export. Some one hundred papers were withdrawn.[32]

Shortly after the incident, the National Academy of Sciences Panel on Scientific Communication and National Security published a report on the application of controls to scientific communication.[33] The panel had been asked to suggest how to balance competing national objectives so as to best serve the general welfare. It concluded that the problem of technology transfer was real, that there was indeed substantial leakage of information damaging to national security, but that universities and open scientific communication had little direct impact on the problem. The panel also concluded that government restrictions on the free flow of information would damage scientific and economic advances as well as military progress, and that national security is more likely to be enhanced through open scientific communication than through a policy of secrecy controls.

Yet, the fact remains that American defense and foreign policy in the 1980s includes systematic restrictions on the exchange of scientific information. The government has imposed new restrictions extending control over information of potential military use, and it has reinterpreted existing laws to include broader categories of technical information. Although these restrictions have met recently with outrage from scientists who seem to feel that they represent unprecedented constraints, a long-time observer of government-science relationships, Harold Green, was surprised about the flap. Green, a lawyer specializing in atomic energy restrictions, claims that the so-called novel or unprecedented efforts by government officials to interfere with private research and publication have always been there; it is just that the scientific community has been "anaesthetized and acquiescent," prudently reluctant to challenge national policy.[34]

More surprising than the flap over growing restrictions on the scientific enterprise are the simultaneous appeals for Defense Department support of academic training and research. Such funding increases the scale of research in precisely those areas that are most vulnerable to national security controls. While appalled at such controls and fearful of their effect on teaching and research, scientists, and even the NAS Panel, are not questioning the implication of increased military support of academic research. Yet this support will influence the direction of university research and may have dire implications for the autonomy of science in academia.

7. Negotiating the Control of Scientific Information

The relationship between science and society has often been described as a marriage. Such a relationship implies shared assumptions and mutual trust, and, therefore, the adequacy of ad hoc arrangements with respect to such critical issues as the ownership and control of research.[1] The marriage, however, is over. In fact, one might better describe the current connection as a "negotiated treaty," or perhaps an affair of convenience, based less on trust than on mutually recognized self-interest and interdependence. In this new relationship, scientific autonomy and freedom of inquiry, once taken for granted as undisputed rights, are more accurately viewed as products of negotiated agreement and exchange.

The policies that provided federal patronage for science with minimal public control resulted from negotiations that began after World War II. On the premise that what is good for science is good for the public, science became, according to Harvard political scientist Don Price, "the only set of institutions for which tax funds are appropriated almost on faith and under concordats which protect the autonomy, if not the cloistered calm, of the laboratory."² Unusual in its provisions for scientific autonomy, the postwar contract has been subject to continued reevaluation and debate.

The disputes over the ownership of scientific information and control of research that are described in the preceding chapters suggest the fragility of this contract and how persistent the pressures to renegotiate the terms of scientific autonomy have become. The very diversity of these disputes suggest their ubiquitous and systemic character. They arise in very different situations, but they are neither discrete nor unusual events. They all bear on questions of secrecy in science, on the policies and practices that govern the public disclosure of technical information, and on the freedom of the scientist to control the disclosure and dissemination of research.

That these questions provoke such intense political debate reflects significant changes in the traditional understanding of science and its relation to the public good. Scientific knowledge has become, in effect, a commodity, vulnerable to commercial interests, public demands, and military controls. The disputes reflect recurrent changes in governmental policies toward research today in the direction of greater restrictions on the free flow of information. And they reflect structural changes in the profession of science—changes that themselves are a source of tension as the norms and expectations of the scientific community conflict with current economic and political realities.

Science in a Changing Social and Political Context

As the scope of research has expanded, so too have the

clinical, industrial, and policy applications of scientific knowledge. In a knowledge-based economy, science has become integrally related to human welfare, to the shape and quality of everyday life. A variety of interest groups sees the relevance of research to social, political, or legal decisions, and its value for commercial and military affairs. In this context, scientific knowledge is subject to competing claims that alter traditional assumptions about the control of scientific ideas.

The politics of knowledge—the question of who owns and controls the distribution and use of scientific information—is by no means a new issue. The debate over the hydrogen bomb, the arbitrary practice of blacklisting during the 1950s, and the tensions over release of the "Pentagon papers" during the Vietnam War all involved attempts by various groups to assert control of knowledge. Protecting the confidentiality of research sources has been a persistent source of contention. So too have been the efforts to limit military classification of technical information. The liaisons formed between universities and government or industry sponsors have also raised questions about the control of research. The military support of research on campus, the consulting arrangements of faculty, the expansion of engineering schools, and the dual responsibilities of land-grant colleges have all forced continued reevaluation of the public role of academic and scientific institutions. The pure scientist working in an ivory tower has long been extinct.

A number of factors have converged in the 1980s to intensify debates about ownership and control in the research enterprise. First, scientific knowledge itself, as well as its application, is sought for its commercial and military value. The lead time between discovery and application has been substantially reduced, and in many fields, the distinctions between basic and applied research are breaking down. Thus ideas themselves have increasingly become a focus of intellectual property disputes.

Powerful economic incentives for the commercial exploitation of scientific ideas have encouraged these trends. Changes in patent law and other specific legislative efforts to promote innovation have provided the impetus for increasing industrial investment in research. Venture capital has been available for the commercial development of scientific ideas. Lucrative Defense Department contracts are increasingly available for the support of military research and the training of technical personnel. In a fragile economy, universities are forced into new income-producing arrangements with both industry and the military. However, while providing research support, these arrangements also raise proprietary problems. In particular, the growing dependence on both military and industrial support distorts negotiating relationships and weakens the position of the scientific community as it bargains to maintain its freedom from external controls.

The most explicit threats to scientific autonomy are changing federal policies concerning both national defense and foreign technological competition. Governmental actions under the administration of President Ronald Reagan have reversed the trend toward more open communication and freedom of information that has been gradually implemented over the past thirty years. Proposed amendments to the Freedom of Information Act (FOIA), new regulations inhibiting exchange of technical information, a new and restrictive executive order on security classification, sanctions against whistleblowers, changes in export controls—and budget cuts restricting the collection and dissemination of data—all form a coherent and consistent pattern of information control. These economic and political changes have spilled over into the research environment, where changes in professional relationships are taking place within the scientific community.

Many fields of science today depend on sophisticated and costly technology and on teams of specialized technical personnel. This situation contributes to changes in the nature of the scientific profession, the competitive process of research, and the relationship between science and the public and private sectors. Physicist John Ziman has described these changes as "a social process of collectivization and instrumentalization in science," with less and less autonomy and a decline in the relative importance of internal criteria for the selection of research priorities.[3] External criteria of social or commercial merit increasingly bear on research—a situation parodied by the fictitious scientist Grant Swinger who perpetually shifts his research according to the possibility of support. Advertised positions often require scientists who apply to demonstrate "proven ability to generate grant support," in effect setting new professional standards that recognize the dependence of the scientific enterprise on external funds.

The profession of science has also acquired a new diversity of roles. Scientists serve as advisors to policymakers, consultants to government and private enterprise, expert witnesses in the courts, technical administrators and bureaucrats, social critics, popularizers, advocates for public interest groups, and above all, educators. These multiple roles are intrinsic to the scientific enterprise. Yet they involve political or economic relationships that necessarily affect the behavior of sci-

entists, as obligations of responsibility, external accountability, and institutional loyalty compete with traditional
expectations of professional sovereignty and autonomous
control. Indeed, as historian Gerald Holton observed, "If
science ever was a charismatic profession dominated by
abstract spirits, those days are gone forever."[4]

Science, Sovereignty, and Secrecy

Changes in the political and economic relations of
science have added new dimensions to long-standing
conflicts between autonomy and external control. Industrial and military support bring opportunity, but also
impose constraints. Scientists respond to constraints by
trying to protect their autonomy. Maintaining an atti-
tude of "prudential acquiescence"[5] in the face of conflicting pressures, they have yet to organize a coherent and
collective response to external demands. This is illustrated by the surprisingly ad hoc responses to the challenges to scientific sovereignty described in this book.

So long as scientists react to each challenge as a
unique event, contradictions are inevitable. We have
seen scientists warn again and again that external constraints will "chill" the progress of science, but they
apply the metaphor in conflicting ways. Proprietary restrictions on open communication resulting from commercial competition would have a "chilling effect" on
research, but so too would restrictions on the entrepreneurial ventures of scientists who want to market
their research. National security constraints on the communication of science would "chill" progress in some of
the most advanced scientific and technical areas, but so
too would inadequate military support for costly research. Early disclosure of data because of FOIA requests

would have a "chilling effect," but so too would restrictions on the disclosure of data bearing on public health and safety.

Contradictions are manifest in frequently inconsistent attempts to maintain control over data. Scientists seek statutory protection from the disclosure requirements of the FOIA, but in doing so, they help to weaken legislation that encourages the open exchange of information. Proposals to amend the FOIA explicitly exempt research, along with trade secrets, from compulsory disclosure, but this exemption may also restrict the open exchange of technical information so valued by scientists themselves.

To ward off external controls, scientists attempt to sharpen distinctions between basic and applied research, but in other contexts they emphasize the futility, indeed, the impossibility of making such distinctions, saying, "There is only one science." Understandably outraged by the extension of national defense restraints, scientists also seek greater support of research from the military agencies, ignoring its potential for still greater security controls. The outrage about the threats to open communication imposed by government review sharply contrasts with the relative absence of concern about similar industrial constraints.

These contradictory positions are inherently vulnerable to attack. In a public statement on the need for military controls, Admiral Bobby Inman pointed out the inconsistencies in the vigorous resistance to national security restraints.:

> Scientists' blanket claims of freedom are somewhat disingenuous in light of the arrangements that academics routinely make with private corporate sources of funding. For example, academi-

cians do not seem to have any serious difficulty with restrictions on publications that arise from corporate concern for trade secret protection.[6]

The persistence of such contradictions reflects profound ambivalence among scientists about the role of secrecy in research. On the one hand, the norms of scientific behavior require open communication and the sharing of data as both a moral imperative and a pragmatic need. Science as an institution has been considered part of the public domain, its growth and development intrinsically tied to open communication.[7] Secrecy is believed to be damaging to science: an obstacle to creativity, to the cumulative work necessary for progress, and to the system of peer review necessary to maintain the quality and integrity of scientific work. Thus, scientists have often struggled against security restrictions, loyalty oaths, extension of security classification, trade secrecy, or other measures that would restrict communication.

On the other hand, the moral outrage expressed in response to such restrictions often has a certain ritualistic quality, for secrecy is a powerful technique used by all groups, including scientists, to protect information and to maintain autonomy and control. Maintaining secrecy is rational and instrumental behavior.[8] Scientists employ secrecy to support their position in priority disputes, to protect their work from plagiarism, to divert competition, to avoid external interference, and to ensure the accuracy of results before disclosure.[9] Many of the cases described in this book show how scientists themselves control information in order to protect their data from FOIA requests or subpoenas, and even from colleagues when commercial interests are at stake.

In the competitive culture of science, struggles involving secrecy are not aberrant but endemic, "an integral part of the social relations between scientists."[10] This is apparent in the long history of priority disputes, from Galileo, who struggled to defend his priority over the invention of the geometric compass and the telescope, to Newton, who once called natural philosophy "an impertinently litigious lady" and fought with Leibnitz over the invention of the calculus, to Hooke, who has been called the universal claimant.

Balancing secrecy against the open exchange of ideas has always been part of the culture of science,[11] but the economic incentives now at stake have upset the traditional equilibrium by further encouraging protection of data and ideas. Ambivalence about secrecy is reflected in the contradictory responses to proprietary disputes and in the difficulty of coming to grips with the challenges imposed by expanded governmental restrictions on the flow of scientific ideas.

Negotiation and Accommodation

Efforts to negotiate proprietary disputes have been encumbered by the ubiquitous tendency of all competing groups to justify their claims to intellectual property in the peremptory terms of "rights." Scientists claim the "right" to control the production and dissemination of their research results, arguing that autonomy is necessary to maintain the integrity of research, to carry out their ethical obligations to research subjects, to avoid the misinterpretation of premature data, and to protect their "stock-in-trade." They therefore seek judicial, administrative, and statutory protection to maintain these rights.[12] However, those invoking the FOIA argue that the "right to know" is an essential condition of democracy and the very basis through which the citizen can control the conduct of public affairs. Government agencies claim their "right" to information to carry out their mandated obligations to ensure responsible use of federal funds, to meet policy goals, or to maintain national security or law enforcement in the public interest. Commercial interests claim the "right" to maintain confidentiality in order to reap the benefits of the research they support.

The proprietary disputes over scientific information touch on basic social and political values. In the words of Congressman George Brown, "They stem from the conflicting demands of the most fundamental matters in public policy: the security of the nation and its economic well-being versus the right of citizens to privacy, assembly, free speech, travel and freedom from unwarranted government intervention."[13] However, the discourse on rights only exacerbates conflict as various groups deal with their own needs in isolation and therefore in competition.

Rights, as defined by philosopher H. L. H. Hart, are "moral justifications for limiting the freedom of another."[14] They leave little room for accommodation. Each and every claim for control over the results of research may in itself be reasonable, but collectively they are fundamentally incompatible. The public's right of access to information under the FOIA, for example, limits the scientist's right to control the adequacy and integrity of the research process. The legal or policy needs of government limit the scientist's responsibility to respect the confidentiality of his sources. The right of the individual researcher to compete in his field conflicts with the values of open communication in science. And the right of research sponsors to control the work they support conflicts with the right of scientists to circulate their data and ideas.

Appeals to rights have become a reflex in this society where we debate the rights of the fetus, the rights of future generations, or the right to die. Correlative with obligations, rights may be a practical condition to fulfill certain tasks. For example, law enforcement agencies, obliged to maintain law and order, claim the right to information in order to do their job. Other claims to rights are based on the utilitarian argument that certain rights are valued because they maximize the public interest. Scientists, for example, argue that the acquisition of knowledge is so important for the long-term interests of society that the autonomous pursuit of knowledge must override other objectives. Others base their claims to rights on a libertarian premise that individual autonomy is an ultimate value in itself.

Whatever the reason for appealing to rights, the language itself often contributes to the confusion of moral categories with practical or strategic goals. In some disputes over intellectual property, claims to rights are little more than ad hoc responses to competitive situations, a means to avoid accountability or to protect research against external pressures whether or not these pressures are justified in larger policy terms. Indeed, the rhetoric of rights may be simply a way to elevate instrumental behavior to the level of a moral imperative, leaving little room for negotiation and accommodation.[15]

If the autonomy of science is to be understood as a negotiated contract rather than an inalienable right, several principles of accommodation must follow. Negotiations must leave room for compromise. Thus the concept of rights must be understood not as morally imperative but as socially defined; delimited by time, place, and situation; and correlated with responsibility. At one time it was acceptable for Americans to claim rights over their slaves, and gold miners in the Fiji Islands found it reasonable to claim the right to have a sex break at lunch because they were too tired for sex in the evening.[16] The changing social context of science today has brought new situations where traditional assumptions about the freedom of science and the control of scientific knowledge are no longer fully accepted. Rhetorical claims to scientific freedom based on these assumptions can only obstruct negotiation.

Viable negotiating relationships also require a base of mutual understanding and shared definitions. Negotiations over the control of research require some consensus about what is "legitimate" or "good" research that is worthy of protection. Should the criteria for protection of research be based on the credentials of scientists, or the sources of research support? On the methodology of the research in question, or the social purposes to which it may be applied? Scientists, bargaining for administrative or statutory protection, must clarify the cognitive and pragmatic dimensions of science. Is science the pursuit of truth or the pursuit of useful knowledge? A carefully disciplined process or a professional and instrumental activity? Is science to be pursued because of its intrinsic value, or is it of value because of its potential applications?

Negotiated definitions must also clarify such vague concepts as "national security" and "technological progress," concepts routinely used to justify science policy decisions. Is there indeed a fundamental conflict between national security and the tradition of open communication in science? Or does this tradition of openness ultimately contribute to the technological progress so necessary for the effective security of the nation?

Finally, if scientists are to establish a viable and responsible bargaining position in intellectual property disputes, they must deal more consistently with questions of secrecy in science. Secrecy is the pivotal issue in these disputes. Consistency on this issue is clearly difficult, because of the many social pressures that encourage secrecy: intense professional competition, the quest for priority in commercially profitable fields, concerns about the effect of premature disclosure of data, and the scramble for research funds. However, inconsistency can lead to inadvertent collaboration with some of the more pernicious trends in recent policies of information control.

The imposition of secrecy on scientific research for whatever reason—national security, strategic advantage, technological competition, or proprietary interest—threatens both science and the public interest. A consistent and responsible position on the control of information is in the best interests of scientists, government, industry, and the entire community of interests involved in the effort to renegotiate relationships between science and the public—to redefine those norms of communication and disclosure that were established when science was a different social enterprise.

References
and Notes

Chapter 1

1. Louis Pasteur, quoted in National Science Board, *Only One Science*, 12th Annual Report (Washington: GPO, 1981), i.

2. Thomas Moss, "A Congressional Viewpoint on Innovation Through Technology," in *Entrepreneurship and Innovation*, vol. 1 of the *Chief Executive Development Series* (Washington: Paterson & Co., 1980), 31.

3. See cases discussed in Dorothy Nelkin, ed., *Controversy* (Beverly Hills: Sage, 1979).

4. *Webster's New International Dictionary*, 2d ed., s.v. "intellectual property."

5. National Commission on Research, *Funding Mechanisms* (Washington, 1980). Beginning in the early 1970s, NIH increased its use of contracts as part of its "war" against cancer and heart disease. This created widespread concern among scientists about increased management and control in areas of research needing the flexibility to generate new ideas. NIH backed down, making less use of the contract system.

6. Percy Bridgeman, quoted in G. Piel, "Science Policy as Cargo Cult" (Lecture presented at the 31st National Conference on Advancement of Research, Albuquerque, N.M., 5 October 1977).

7. Robert K. Merton, "Priorities in Scientific Discovery," in *The Sociology of Science*, Robert K. Merton, ed. (Chicago: University of Chicago Press, 1973), 273.

8. Frank Horton, chairman of the Commission on Federal Paperwork, quoted in House Committee on Government Operations, *Lack of Guidelines for Federal Contract and Grant Data*, 95th Cong., 2d sess. (Washington: GPO, 1978), 3.

9. I will focus on the more controversial proprietary questions, excluding those areas of military research and applied industrial work that are indisputably subject either to trade secrecy or military classification.

Chapter 2

1. Nicholas Wade, "University and Drug Firm Battle Over Billion Dollar Gene," *Science* 209 (26 September 1980), 1492–94.

2. Nicholas Wade, "La Jolla Biologists Troubled by Midas Factor," *Science* 213 (7 August 1981), 623–28.

3. Russell Doolittle, quoted in Wade, "Biologists Troubled," 628.

4. Donald Kennedy, "Health Research: Can Utility and Quality Co-exist?" (Lecture given at the University of Pennsylvania, 6 December 1980).

5. Harvey Brooks, *Technology and Society in the 1980s* (Paris: OECD, 1981), 27.

6. *Diamond v. Chakrabarty* 447 U.S. (16 June 1980), 303–322.

7. "New Patent Policy Bill Gathers Congressional Support," *Bioscience* 29 (May 1979), 281.

8. For a discussion of Public Law 96–517 and its implications, see Advisory Committee to the Director of NIH,

Cooperative Research Relationships with Industry (Washington: NIH, October 1981).

9. Joan Robinson, *The Accumulation of Capital* (London: Macmillan, 1956), 87.

10. Letter from Arthur Bueche to S. Dedijer, quoted in S. Dedijer, "Management Intelligence and Secrecy Management," in Manfred Schmutzer, *Technische Innovation* (Wien: Interdisziplinares Forschungszentrum, 1979), 119.

11. For the intent of patenting, see Russell B. Stevenson, Jr., *Corporations and Information* (Baltimore: Johns Hopkins University Press, 1980). For concerns about the effect of patenting on secrecy, see Advisory Committee to the Director of NIH, *Research Relationships*.

12. David F. Noble, *America by Design: Science, Technology, and the Rise of Corporate Capitalism* (New York: Alfred A. Knopf, 1977), chap. 2.

13. Ibid., 141.

14. Vannevar Bush, *Science: The Endless Frontier* (Washington: GPO, July 1945).

15. Advisory Committee on Industrial Policy, *Domestic Policy Review* (Washington: U.S. Department of Commerce, 1979), 205.

16. National Commission on Research, *Industry and the Universities: Developing Cooperative Research Relationships in the National Interest* (Washington, August 1980). Copies of this document can be obtained by writing to Dr. Cornelius J. Pings, Provost, University of Southern California.

17. Bernard L. Strehler, "Hayflick–NIH Settlement," *Science* 215 (15 January 1982), 240–42. Constance Holden, "Hayflick Case Settled," *Science* 215 (15 January 1982), 271.

18. Harold Green, "Genetic Technology May Prompt New Legal Regime," *Legal Times of Washington*, 18 January 1982, 17–18. Green argues that as this technology is commercialized, it cannot be absorbed into the traditional framework of patent and trade secrecy law. He finds com-

pelling analogies between genetic technology and atomic energy. Because genetic technology affects social and ethical values and presents unusual risks, it will require unique legal and regulatory institutions.

19. Office of Technology Assessment, *Impacts of Applied Genetics* (Washington: GPO, 1981). The possible applications of genetic manipulation stimulated the development of new biotechnology firms, but their activities are quite varied. Some use biological techniques to improve existing products; others seek to develop new products. The direct manipulation of genetic materials to produce new organisms is only part of this burgeoning industry.

20. Donald Kennedy, "Commercializing University Biomedical Research," *National Association of State Universities and Land Grant Colleges: Ethical and Institutional Impacts* (Testimony before the Subcommittee on Investigations and Oversight, House Committee on Science and Technology, 97th Cong., 1st sess., 8 June 1981).

21. For a discussion of these arrangements, see *Hearings on Commercialization of Academic Biomedical Research*, Subcommittee on Science, Research, and Technology, House Committee on Science and Technology, 97th Cong., 1st sess., 7 June 1981.

22. Letter from the Comptroller General of the United States to the Hon. Albert Gore, Jr., Committee on Science and Technology, U.S. House of Representatives, 16 October 1981, cited in *Hearings on Commercialization of Academic Biomedical Research*, op. cit.

23. Ibid.

24. Colin Norman, "MIT Agonizes over Links with Research Unit," *Science* 214 (13 October 1981), 416–17.

25. Biologist Sheldon Penman, quoted in *The New York Times*, 15 November 1981, sec. 4.

26. Derek Bok, "Business and the Academy," *Harvard Magazine* 83 (May/June 1981), 23–25.

27. See, for example, the discussion in the Minutes of the

43rd meeting of the Advisory Committee to the Director of NIH on 8–9 June 1981, in Advisory Committee, *Research Relationships*, 265–82.

28. Donald Kennedy, "Commercializing University Biomedical Research."

29. Derek Bok, "Business and the Academy."

30. A former commissioner of the FDA, Jere Goyan, argues that if universities become heavily involved in patenting new products using gene splicing techniques, scientists will forfeit their role as independent advisors. Agencies such as the FDA would have problems finding consultants who do not have a conflict of interest. See *Science* 215 (22 January 1982), 382.

31. Don K. Price, "Endless Frontier of Bureaucratic Morass," in Gerald Holton and Robert S. Morison, eds., *Limits of Scientific Inquiry* (New York: W. W. Norton, 1979), 76.

32. Karl T. Compton, "Science and Prosperity," *Science 80* (2 November 1934), 393–94.

33. See, for example, Gilbert Omenn, "University/Industry Research Linkages: Arrangements Between Faculty Members and Their Institutions" (Paper delivered at the 1982 Annual Meeting of the American Association for the Advancement of Science, Washington, D.C., 6 January 1982).

34. Donald Kennedy, *Business, Science, and the Universities* (Address to the Committee for Corporate Support of Private Universities in New York, 20 May 1981). This address is available as a booklet from the president's office at Stanford University.

Chapter 3

1. University Group Diabetes Program, "A Study of the Effects of Hypoglycemic Agents on Vascular Complications in Patients with Vascular, Adult-Onset Diabetes," *Diabetes*, Supp. 2 (December 1970), 747–830. A list of 27 articles in which this research is discussed and a review of

the case appears in the *Federal Register* 40 (7 July 1975), 28587–95.

2. *Forsham v. Califano*, 587 F.2d 1128 (D.C. Cir., 1978).

3. Ibid., 1129.

4. Ibid., 1128–40.

5. Ibid., 1140–49.

6. *Forsham v. Harris*, 445 U.S. 169 (1980).

7. *St. Paul's Benevolent Education and Missionary Institute v. U.S.*, 506 F Supp 822 (N.D. Ga. 1980).

8. Ibid.

9. *Dow Chemical v. Dr. James Allen*, U.S. District Court, Western District of Wisconsin, 80–C–C33, 12 June 1980.

10. Ibid.

11. *Dow Chemical v. Dr. James Allen*, U.S. Court of Appeals, 7th Circuit, 80–2013. Decision, 25 February 1982.

12. Ibid.

13. For discussion of the evolution of the Freedom of Information Act, see Harold Relyea, "Freedom of Information, Privacy, and Official Secrecy: The Evolution of Federal Government Information Policy Concepts," *Social Indicators Research* 7 (1980), 137–56, and "The Provision of Government Information: The Federal FOIA Experience," *Canadian Public Administration* 20 (Summer 1977), 317–341.

14. Bowen I. Hosford, "FOIA Requests at NIH, 1975–1979" (Washington: National Institutes of Health, 1980).

15. For example, an estimated 90 percent of the FOIA requests to the Food and Drug Administration came from competing drug companies. A number of consulting firms have been formed to obtain information under the act; their clients are corporations seeking to obtain knowledge from competitors.

16. Robert S. Gordon, Jr., "Data Control Considerations Unique to Clinical Trials" (Paper presented at the 1982

Annual Meeting of the American Association for the Advancement of Science, Washington, D.C., 5 January 1982).

17. Robert L. Levine, *Ethics and Regulation of Clinical Research* (Baltimore: Urban and Schwarzenberg, 1981), 132–35; D. H. Cowan, "Scientific Design, Ethics, and Monitoring: Review of Randomized Clinical Trials," *IRB: A Review of Human Subjects Research* 2 (9 November 1980), 1–4.

18. James H. Jones, *Bad Blood: The Tuskegee Syphilis Experiment* (New York: The Free Press, 1981).

19. Letter from Robert M. Bock, dean of the University of Wisconsin Graduate School, to John T. Edsall, Frederick Robbins, and Philip Handler, 13 January 1981.

20. Letter from John T. Edsall to Steven C. Underwood, assistant attorney general of the state of Wisconsin, 3 February 1981.

21. Restatement (2nd) of Torts Explanatory Notes §757, Comment b, at 5 (1939). (St. Paul: American Law Institute; see also annual reports and supplements).

22. Russell B. Stevenson, Jr., *Corporations and Information* (Baltimore: Johns Hopkins University Press, 1980). The Commission on Federal Paperwork cites 90 provisions of law protecting business information. See *Confidentiality and Privacy* (Washington: GPO, 1977), 26.

23. Attorney general's memorandum on the public information section of the Administrative Procedures Act, June 1967, 34.

24. *Washington Research Project Inc. v. HEW*, 504 F.2d 238 (D.C. Cir., 1974).

25. Ibid., at 244.

26. Ibid., at 244–45.

27. Senate Bill S.1730, as amended to Section 552 (b) (4) of the FOIA, 14 December 1981, 97th Cong., 1st sess. (S. 1730 was brought before the Senate in December 1982 but died on the Senate Calendar, 22 December 1982).

28. Joe S. Cecil and Eugene Griffin, "Legal Issues in Obtaining Access to Data," in Robert F. Boruch et al., "Access to Research Data," draft report to the National Research Council Committee on National Statistics, 1981.

29. Robert C. Denicola, "Copyright in Collections of Facts," *Columbia Law Review* 81, no. 3 (April 1981), 516–42.

30. National Commission for the Protection of Human Subjects of Biomedical and Behavioral Research, *Report on Disclosure of Research Information under the FOIA* (Washington: GPO, 1977).

31. Ethics Advisory Board of the Department of Health and Human Services, *Report on Request of the NIH for Limited Exemption from the Freedom of Information Act,* (Washington, 7 March 1980).

Chapter 4

1. The description of Popkin's ordeal is summarized from James D. Carroll, "Confidentiality of Social Science Research Sources and Data: The Popkin Case," *PS*, Summer 1973, 268–80.

2. House Committee on Government Operations, *Lack of Guidelines for Federal Contract and Grant Data*, Report no. 29 (Washington: GPO, 1978), 9–10.

3. Letter from the Assistant Secretary for Planning and Evaluation to the AAAS Committee on Scientific Freedom and Responsibility, 24 November 1975.

4. Donald McTavish et al., Postscript of February 1975, Report to NSF on Grant NM–44386, University of Minnesota, 6 December 1975.

5. Kathleen Bond, "Confidentiality and the Protection of Human Subjects in Social Science Research," *The American Sociologist* 13 (3 August 1978), 144–52.

6. Seymour M. Lipset, testimony in U.S. District Court for the *District of Massachusetts v. John Doe*, Memorandum of Law of Samuel L. Popkin in Support of his Motion for Protective Order, 27 October 1971, 13.

7. James Q. Wilson, in ibid., 9.

8. These and other cases are described by James Carroll and Charles Knerr in "Statement for the Federal Privacy Study Commission," *Public Hearings on Research and Statistical Records*, 5–6 January 1977.

9. James D. Carroll and Charles Knerr, "Myron Farber, *The New York Times*, and American Science," unpublished manuscript, 18 August 1978. (Available through James D. Carroll, The Brookings Institution, Washington, D.C.).

10. Carroll and Knerr, "Statement for the Federal Privacy Study Commission."

11. For example, the Comprehensive Drug Abuse, Prevention, and Control Act of 1970 (42 U.S.C. sec. 242 (a) 1970) authorizes the secretary of the Department of Health and Human Services to allow scientists engaged in drug research to protect the anonymity of research subjects and explicitly establishes testimonial privilege for such researchers. Statutory protection of research information is also provided by the Privacy Act of 1974, the Public Health Services Act (as amended in 1974), the Crime Control Act of 1973, and the Drug Abuse Office and Treatment Act (as amended in 1974). For a review of legal assurances of confidentiality, see Robert F. Boruch and Joe S. Cecil, *Assuring the Confidentiality of Social Research Data* (Philadelphia: University of Pennsylvania Press, 1979), 225–62. For a review of federal regulations, see N. Reatig, "Confidentiality Certificates: A Measure of Privacy Protection," *IRB: A Review of Human Subjects Research* 1, no. 3 (May 1979), 1–4, 12.

12. Privacy Act (Public Law 93–579), 5 U.S.C. 552a 1974.

13. Leon Gordis and Ellen Gold, "Privacy, Confidentiality, and the Use of Medical Records in Research," *Science* 207 (11 January 1980), 153–56.

14. Boruch and Cecil, *Confidentiality of Data*, 60–92.

15. Paul Nejelski, "The Prosecutor and the Researcher," *Social Problems* 21, no. 1 (Summer 1973), 3–21. See also

Nejelski, "A Researcher's Shield Statute," Report to the Committee on Federal Agency Evaluation Research, National Research Council, National Academy of Sciences, Washington, D.C., 1975.

16. *Branzburg v. Hayes*, 408 U.S. 665 (1972).

17. Ibid., at 705, 706.

18. Privacy of Research Records Bill, S. 867 (4 April 1979) and H.R. 3409 (3 April 1979), 96th Cong., 1st sess.

19. Privacy of Medical Records Bill, H.R. 5935 (16 November 1979) and S. 865 (4 April 1979), 96th Cong., 1st sess.

20. Boruch and Cecil, *Confidentiality of Data*, 81–83.

Chapter 5

1. See letter from Robert Alvarez, Environmental Policy Institute, in *Science* 216 (30 April 1982), 486–63, for a list of published papers.

2. U.S. Department of Energy, "Investigation Report," 44–2–445, 5 May 1978. U.S. House of Representatives, Hearings before the House Committee on Interstate and Foreign Commerce, Subcommittee on Health and the Environment, 8 February 1978, 95th Cong., 2d sess. "Effects of Radiation on Health," vol. 1 (Washington: GPO, 1979).

3. Testimony by Thomas F. Mancuso in ibid., 523–33.

4. Thomas F. Mancuso, "Radiation Exposures of Hanford Workers Dying from Cancer and Other Causes," *Health Physics* 33 (1977), 369–84.

5. U.S. Department of Energy, "Investigation Report."

6. Constance Holden, "Scientist with Unpopular Data Loses Job," *Science* 210 (14 November 1980), 749–50. See also letter from Baslow's employer, John P. Lawler, in *Science* 211 (27 February 1981), 875–76. See also Arthur N. Oakes, "Protecting the Rights of Whistleblowers and the Accused in Federally Supported Biomedical Research," in

President's Commission for the Study of Ethical Problems in Medicine and Biomedical and Behavioral Research, *Whistleblowing in Biomedical Research* (Washington: GPO, 1982), 111–42.

7. Holden, "Scientist Loses Job."

8. See Alan Westin, *Whistleblowing: Loyalty and Dissent in the Corporation* (New York: McGraw Hill, 1981).

9. Marjorie Sun, "A Firing over Formaldehyde," *Science* 213 (7 August 1981), 630–31.

10. Peter Raven-Hansen, "Do's and Don'ts for Whistleblowers," *Technology Review*, May 1980, 34–38.

11. See William Broad, "Fraud and the Structure of Science," *Science* 212 (10 April 1981), 137–44; Broad, "Harvard Delays in Coping with Fraud," *Science* 215 (29 January 1982), 478, 482; Broad, "Coping with Fraud," *Science* 215 (29 January 1982), 479.

12. Arthur N. Oakes, "Rights of Whistleblowers."

13. Albert Gore, Jr., opening statement in *Hearings on Fraud and Falsification of Data*, House Committee on Science and Technology, Subcommittee on Investigations and Oversight, 97th Cong., 1st sess., (Washington: GPO, 31 March 1981), 1.

14. Judith Swazey and Stephen Scher, "The Whistleblower as a Deviant Professional: Professional Norms and Responses to Fraud in Clinical Research," in President's Commission, *Whistleblowing in Biomedical Research*.

15. Michael Brown, "Setting Occupational Health Standards: The Vinyl Chloride Case," in Dorothy Nelkin, ed., *Controversy* (Beverly Hills: Sage, 1979), 125–43.

16. *The New York Times*, 23 April 1979.

17. Thomas O. McGarity and Sidney A. Shapiro, "The Trade Secret Status of Health and Safety Testing Information," *Harvard Law Review* 93 (5 March 1980), 831–888.

18. R. J. Smith, "Tight Screening Plan for EPA Data," *Science* 213 (18 September 1981), 1345–46.

19. Arnold Relman, "The Patient and the Press," *Bryn Mawr Alumni Bulletin*, Fall 1981, 2–5.

20. Sidney M. Wolfe, "Peer Review and the Public's Right to Know" (Paper delivered at the 1982 Annual Meeting of the American Association for the Advancement of Science, Washington, D.C., 6 January 1982).

21. Raven-Hansen, "Do's and Don'ts for Whistleblowers."

22. John T. Edsall, "Two Aspects of Scientific Responsibility," *Science* 212 (3 April 1981), 13.

23. Civil Service Reform Act, Public Law 95–454 (1978).

24. Rosemary Chalk et al., "Professional Ethics Activities in the Scientific and Engineering Societies," *AAAS Professional Ethics Project Report*, December 1980.

25. Rosemary Chalk, "The Miners' Canary," *Bulletin of the Atomic Scientists*, February 1982, 22. (At one time miners took canaries, which are highly sensitive to methane gas, into the mines to warn them when the deadly gas was accumulating.)

Chapter 6

1. Stephen H. Unger, "The Growing Threat of Government Secrecy," *Technology Review*, February/March 1982, 31–39, 84–85.

2. Mary M. Cheh, "*The Progressive* Case and the Atomic Energy Act: Waking to the Dangers of Government Information Controls," *George Washington Law Review* 48 (2 January 1980), 163–210.

3. Erwin Knoll, "Born Secret," *The Progressive*, May 1979, 15. *The Progressive*'s position was endorsed by the publishers of journals as diverse as *The Nation*, *Harpers'*, *Atlantic Monthly*, *Scientific American*, *Science for the People*, and *Mother Jones*.

4. See Harold C. Relyea, "The Evolution of Government Information Security Classification Policy: A Brief Overview," in Senate Committee on Government Operations,

Hearings on Government Secrecy, 93rd Cong., 2d sess. (Washington: GPO, 1974), 842–84.

5. Harold C. Relyea, "Information, Secrecy, and Atomic Energy," unpublished manuscript, 1980. See also Harold P. Green, "Information Control Under the Atomic Energy Act" (Paper presented at the 1982 Annual Meeting of the American Association for the Advancement of Science, Washington, D.C., 7 January 1982); an abbreviated version of this paper was published in *New York University Review of Law and Social Change*, 1980–1981, 265–286.

6. J. Newman and B. Miller, *The Control of Atomic Energy* (New York: Whittlesey House, 1948), 208.

7. ITAR, 22 C.F.R.§121.01 (1954) Arms Export Control Act, 22 USC §2778 (1976).

8. Export Administration Act 50 USC, App. §2402 (Amended, 1979).

9. U.S. Department of Defense, *Soviet Military Power*, (Washington: GPO, September 1980), 80–81.

10. Correspondence between the deputy secretary of Defense, Frank Carlucci, and the executive officer of the American Association for the Advancement of Science, William D. Carey, *Science* 215 (8 January 1982), 139–41.

11. The unsigned report was apparently written in response to hearings held by the House Committee on Science and Technology on the impact of national security considerations on science and technology, 29 March 1982. The report was published in April 1982 and is available from the Central Intelligence Agency, Washington, D.C.

12. For a review of these restrictions, see Linda Lubrano, "National and International Politics in US-USSR Scientific Cooperation," *Social Studies of Science* 11 (4 November 1981), 451–80.

13. 15 C.F.R. 379.1 (b)(2).

14. The following are excerpts from a letter and questionnaire

sent by the Department of State to universities hosting Chinese scholars in July 1981:

Dear Sir or Madam:

The Chinese scholar(s) at your institution is (are) part of an official US-China exchange program which has sponsored more than 2,000 Chinese scholars and students to study in the United States to date. . . . The majority of these officially sponsored Chinese scholars are pursuing studies to acquire scientific or technical expertise urgently needed by China to achieve its modernization goals. The United States fully supports this effort. However, the United States Government is concerned that none of these programs involve the transfer of technical data which is considered critical on export control or national security grounds. U.S. law and regulations require that the Department of State, together with the relevant U.S. agencies, examine in detail those programs which may involve the transfer of such technical data . . . To be responsive to these concerns, the Department of State requests that you complete the enclosed questionnarie for the scholar(s) named above:

(*Selected questions from Questionnaire*)

What is scholar or student's full name?

How long will this scholar or student be at your institution?

What professional trips might this student or scholar be taking?

What major subject areas will be involved in the scholar or student's program? . . . (include information such as research problems and specific experiments).

How will this program be conducted? For example, will the scholar do individual research or joint laboratory research? What research methods and procedures, instruments . . . or specialized equipment may be used during the course of the study program? Will student have access to specialized library collections? Specialized laboratory facilities? Do the procedures or results of the scholar's research program have applications to the production or processing of advanced materials? If so, how? Do the procedures or results have application to the design, development, manufacture, or reconstruction of any specific end item . . . ? How? Do you [the host professor] or your institution have any contacts with industry or government organizations? If so, please list them and indicate whether the foreign visitor will have any access to contract activities.

15. Letter from Keith Powell of the U.S. State Department to William R. Franta, Computer Science Department, University of Minnesota, 30 September 1981, quoted in *The New York Times*, 27 November 1981. (A copy of this letter is in the possession of the author.)

16. C. Peter McGrath, President, University of Minnesota, letter to Keith Powell, U.S. Department of State, 7 December 1981.

17. Public Law 97–90 (1982).

18. Export Administration Regulations §379.1 (a) (1979).

19. See U.S. Department of State, proposed revisions of ITAR, *Federal Register* 45, no. 246 (19 December 1980), 83970–95.

20. Memorandum from the U.S. Department of Justice, Office of Legal Counsel, to the U.S. Department of Commerce, 28 July 1981. Also see the memorandum from the U.S. Department of Justice, Office of Legal Counsel, to the U.S. Department of State on the Proposed Revision of ITAR, 1 July 1981.

21. Executive Order 12356, "National Security Classification," The White House, February 1982.

22. House Committee on Government Operations, *Report on the President's Executive Order on Security Classification* 97th Cong. 2d sess., 16 August 1982 (Washington: GPO, 1982).

23. Bobby R. Inman, "National Security and Technical Information" (Paper delivered at the 1982 Annual Meeting of the American Association for the Advancement of Science, Washington, D.C., 7 January 1982).

24. Note, however, that this is not a point of consensus in the scientific community. Many scientists would like to use

scientific exchanges as a means of leverage to affect human rights in foreign countries.

25. For a discussion of this idea, see Unger, "Threat of Government Secrecy."

26. *Notices of the American Mathematical Society*, vol. 29, no. 2 (1981), 213.

27. Office of the Under Secretary of Defense for Research and Engineering, *Report of the Defense Science Board Task Force on University Responsiveness to National Security Requirements* (Washington: Defense Science Board, January 1982).

28. Dorothy Nelkin, *The University and Military Research* (Ithaca, N.Y.: Cornell University Press, 1972).

29. Office of Under Secretary of Defense for Research and Engineering, *University Responsiveness.*

30. Robert L. Sproull, Testimony on Universities and Defense Preparedness, House Committee on Armed Services, Subcommittee on Research and Development, 97th Cong., 1st sess., 3 April 1981.

31. See, for example, Wil Lepkowski, "Defense Department Boosts Research Funding," *Chemical and Engineering News* 59 (27 April 1981), 14–15.

32. Gina Kolata, "Export Control Threat Disrupts Meeting," *Science* 217 (24 September 1982), 1233–34.

33. National Academy of Sciences, *Scientific Communication and National Security* (Washington: National Academy Press, 1982).

34. Harold P. Green, "Information Control Under the Atomic Energy Act."

Chapter 7

1. William Bevan, "On Getting in Bed with a Lion," *American Psychologist* 35, (September 1980), 779–89.

2. Don K. Price, "The Scientific Establishment," in Robert Gilpin and Christopher Wright, eds., *Scientists and Na-*

tional Policy-making (New York: Columbia University Press, 1964), 20.

3. John Ziman, "What Are the Options: Social Determinants of Personal Research Plans" (Paper presented at the Conference on Scientific Establishments and Hierarchies, Oxford, England, 5 July 1980).

4. Gerald Holton, "From the Endless Frontier to the Ideology of Limits," in Gerald Holton and Robert S. Morison, eds., *Limits of Scientific Inquiry* (New York: Norton, 1979), 229.

5. This concept was developed by Joseph Haberer in *Politics and the Community of Science* (New York: Van Nostrand Reinhold, 1969), 79–97, to describe the relationship between science and politics.

6. Bobby R. Inman, "National Security and Technical information" (Paper presented at the 1982 Annual Meeting of the American Association for the Advancement of Science, Washington, D.C., 7 January 1982).

7. Robert K. Merton, "The Normative Structure of Science," in Merton, *The Sociology of Science* (Chicago: Chicago University Press, 1973), 267–78.

8. Stanton Tefft, "Secrecy as a Social and Political Process," in Stanton Tefft, ed., *Secrecy: A Cross-Cultural Perspective* (New York: Human Sciences Press, 1980), 319–46. See also Max Weber, in *Economy and Society: An Outline of Interpretive Sociology*, Guenther Roth and Claus Wittich, eds. (Berkeley: University of California Press, 1978), 1992–93, for his analysis of how secrecy is used as a means of power and domination.

9. See discussion in Sissela Bok, "Secrecy and Openness in Science: Ethical Considerations," *Science, Technology, and Human Values* 7 (Winter 1982), 32–41.

10. Robert K. Merton, "Priorities in Scientific Discovery," in Merton, *The Sociology of Science*, 286–324.

11. Edward A. Shils, in *Torment of Secrecy* (New York: The Free Press, 1956), 46–47, wrote of the dilemma during the post-war disputes about the hydrogen bomb.

12. Efforts to seek statutory protection are obstructed by vagueness in the definition of "researcher." There are no licensing or certification procedures to provide a formal definition of competence in science, and claims of scientific credibility are open to abuse. For example, religious fundamentalists call themselves "scientific" creationists, thus asserting their own legitimacy as scientists as they challenge the theory of evolution.

13. George Brown, "Administration Policies on Government Control of Information," *Congressional Record*, 97th Cong., 2d sess., 128, no. 16 (25 February 1982), p. H511.

14. Herbert L. Hart, "Are There Any Natural Rights?," *Philosophical Review* 64, no. 2 (April 1955): 175–91.

15. Ruth Macklin, "Moral Concerns and Appeals to Rights and Duties," *Hastings Center Report*, October 1976, 31–38.

16. The Editors, *Hastings Center Report*, October 1976, 33.

Index